THE CASE FOR CULTURE

THE CASE

FOR

CULTURE

HOW TO STOP BEING A SLAVE TO YOUR LAW FIRM, GROW YOUR PRACTICE, AND ACTUALLY BE HAPPY

ERIC FARBER

LIONCREST
PUBLISHING

THE CASE FOR CULTURE
How to Stop Being a Slave to Your Law Firm,
Grow Your Practice, and Actually Be Happy

ISBN   978-1-5445-0587-9 *Hardcover*
       978-1-5445-0585-5 *Paperback*
       978-1-5445-0586-2 *Ebook*
       978-1-5445-0745-3 *Audiobook*

To my wife, Diana

CONTENTS

FOREWORD

As you'll soon discover when you read Eric's history, he probably could've asked any number of NFL Hall of Famers or NBA first-round draft picks to write this foreword. He asked me, though, and I'm honored. I met Eric in 2016 when he asked my company, Crisp Video, to create a premium marketing video for his law firm. In our first conversation, Eric talked about the music artists he'd represented and the class he was teaching at the university. He spoke about everything except law, and it was fascinating.

I quickly understood why Eric was so interested in other industries. Early in his career, he saw that the traditional law firm business model was broken, so he looked elsewhere for solutions. At this point, my company has worked with about a thousand law firms, and we see clients trying to solve problems the same way, over and over again. Law firm owners look to everything except what's happening internally. They spend time and energy examining their marketing problems and attempting to streamline processes.

However, people are at the root of any problem, and it's in people that you'll find any solution. If you can get everybody in your organization aligned, rowing in the same direction, you will solve every other problem. That's what we found in our company. We've grown exponentially over the last several years, became the fastest-growing company in the legal industry, and were listed in the top 10 percent of the fastest-growing companies in the country. We attribute that to our focus on culture.

In that first conversation with Eric, I thought, *This guy gets it*. He understands the business of a law firm and, more importantly, the people aspect of it. He reached outside of the legal world for lessons on culture and applied them to his firm. That's why he's seen such massive growth. His company has increased revenue by more than 1,300 percent over five years and was named to the Inc. 5000 list of fastest growing companies in America.

People look for a magic bullet to make things a little bit better, but Eric and I have both found that improving culture is *transformative*. It's not just something that sounds nice. Culture is everything. It impacts how team members work together, the client experience, and the firm's brand. That means a dialed-in culture provides one of the highest ROI opportunities. There is a direct connection between culture and the ultimate profitability of a business. Law firm owners who do not prioritize culture are at a significant disadvantage. Those who do are the ones who become market leaders.

Since our first meeting, Eric and I have developed a strong friendship. I discovered he's extremely introspective and is always working on himself. He's a lifelong student, continuously learning and looking for unique perspectives. He works from a place of innovation, not competition.

I love that, so I often invite Eric to speak at our annual Game Changers Summit, which is the largest law firm growth conference on Earth. He is consistently one of our highest-rated speakers. People get a lot of value from him. I'm excited for you to share in Eric's value and learn how to transform not just your law firm, but also your life.

Michael Mogill
Crisp Video Group, Founder and CEO
Author of *The Game Changing Attorney*

INTRODUCTION

MISSION LOST

"The path to salvation is narrow and as difficult to walk as a razor's edge."

—W. SOMERSET MAUGHAM

"Is there an N-word for Jews?"

I was shocked when I discovered this question written in an email that an African American employee (who had since left my firm) wrote to a coworker. I was the Jew she wanted to insult.

I was devastated. What was I doing to cause so much anger and vitriol? How had I made an employee feel so alienated? Why didn't my staff like me when I worked so damn hard? It felt soul-destroying. I was exhausted, miserable, and out of touch with my mission and the people around me.

I was working incredibly hard to grow my law firm. I was showing up and doing the work when no one else would. I was canceling on family to spend more hours slaving at my desk. I was marketing, serving clients, doing payroll, worrying about making rent, scrubbing the office kitchen, and locking up at the end of the day.

If you're like most lawyers, you probably don't look at your job as a mission—or, at least, not anymore. You're just trying to do some legal work and earn some money. But consider why most lawyers get into law in the first place. We want to see justice happen. We're driven to speak for people who can't speak for themselves and serve justice to those who would not find it alone. We want to help create the just society our country's founders envisioned.

Over time, lawyers become removed from the ideal of serving justice to clients. We start our own practice to avoid getting sucked into the eighty-hour-a-week treadmill of Big Law, but end up buried in mounds of paperwork, fighting over things that don't matter, and managing people we don't like or respect. We begin to drown under the weight of chasing down clients, struggling to make payroll, and worrying about where next month's rent will come from. When you are drowning and running in scarcity, there isn't time to think about your mission.

We don't have the time or energy to sit back and consider the ways in which we can serve our clients better. How can we bring more justice to the world? How can we be Erin Brockovich? When you are running your own firm, too many hours are dedicated to long, lonely work and wrestling with problems you don't know how to manage. The mission recedes for the sake of survival.

It's no wonder so many lawyers feel unfulfilled, depressed, and isolated. Many of the professional interactions they do have, whether in the course of litigation or negotiation, are highly combative. A huge percentage of lawyers—a rate much higher than that of other professions—battles addictions and mental health issues.

This was the finding in a landmark study in 2016 of more than 10,000 lawyers, conducted by the ABA and Hazelden Betty Ford Foundation. They found that 36 percent of practicing lawyers screened positive for problem drinking, which they defined as "hazardous, harmful, or potentially alcohol dependent." By comparison, only 12 percent of educated workers showed problem drinking, and 15 percent of doctors. The study also identified other issues. Among attorneys, it found significant levels of depression, at 28 percent; anxiety, at 19 percent; and stress, at 23 percent. So many lawyers have lost their north star and look to drugs and alcohol for the fulfillment that work does not bring.

The American Bar Association has begun to address these issues. It now encourages law firms, law schools, and corporate legal departments to pledge to address the mental well-being of lawyers. It suggests having less alcohol at events and talking openly about mental health. This is a start, but it still doesn't take the conversation far enough—or even in the right direction. It doesn't address the culture of billing hours, the isolation and winning without caring about the people behind the work.

I spent most of my career feeling unfulfilled, incredibly lonely, and in constant financial struggle. I found myself battling severe depression. I was never a big drinker; I thought that with my depression, I'd easily become addicted. In struggling to survive, I'd created a toxic culture at my practice, and I had no understanding of how it was all impacting me—let alone the staff who thought their boss was a Jewish N-word.

When I finally figured out how to create a great place to work, not just for my team but for myself, I felt more fulfilled. I became a much, much better boss. My team and I developed a mission to accomplish together. There was no time for depression. Instead of waking up in the night worrying about cash flow, I awoke every morning eager to work. I haven't struggled with depression—or name-calling—in years now. I don't have it all figured out and I stumble often, but our mission always pulls me back to my feet.

STAKEHOLDERS, NOT SHAREHOLDERS

In this book, I'll show you how I accomplished all of this while simultaneously growing my firm's profits in the process. This transformation involved shifting my focus from shareholders to stakeholders.

In a law firm, shareholders are the owners. The stakeholders include all of the people the company touches: the owners, attorneys, staff, clients, vendors and suppliers, their families, and fellow community members. Everybody. Not until recently has there been a shift among business analysts to understand that a company—and a law practice *is* a business—serves not just its shareholders, but all of its stakeholders.

Our law firm employs almost fifty people but serves hundreds of stakeholders. Each employee, as well as my partner and I, goes home at the end of most days with enough strength and vitality to spend time with our families, be good friends, hit the gym, play a great round of golf, and actually enjoy life. Does that mean we don't have hard days? Of course not. They still exist, but now I have the tools to cope with them, and we have created a firm that supports our stakeholders every day. That is incredibly energizing.

More than that, creating this type of environment is essential to success. It is debilitating to work in an environment that leaves you feeling as if the life force has been sucked out of you, leaving you devoid of energy at the end of the day. When you're too drained to do anything other than go home, grab a beer, sit down on the couch, and watch escapist television, there's nothing left for the great little minds you're raising at home or the aging family members you care for. You find yourself stifling your basic human need for connection, society, and safety because you're too tired to tend to them.

I know that as a business owner and leader, it can feel overwhelming to consider all of the stakeholders I've mentioned. In his best-selling book *The Culture Code: The Secrets of Highly Successful Groups*, Daniel Coyle reminds us that the word *culture* comes from the Latin *cultus*, which means *care*. When you begin to see that leading a great company culture is *caring*, you start to see what your job truly is and frankly, it's simple. A leader takes care of their employees. The employees take care of the clients. The clients take care of all of us.

A MORE HUMANE WORKPLACE

The best way to care for these human beings is to create a more humane workplace—which is the essence of great company culture. In this book, you'll discover what company culture looks like in a law firm, and why it must embrace humanity. Naturally, humanity encompasses basic human needs, so you'll learn how to handle—and go beyond—those to create a fulfilling workplace for every employee, not just the attorneys. You'll discover the importance of defining your firm's existing culture (because you do have one, whether or not you're aware of it)—and why, as the leader of your law firm, you must be willing to change before you create a more humane workplace.

You'll learn how to get the right people—those who are already motivated—into the right seats so you can stop managing and start *coaching*. This will allow you to focus on strong processes that develop strong culture, which in turn enables business growth—without more work and stress. When all this comes together, your staff will be unbelievably happy, and, hopefully, un-poachable. Turnover of good people will plummet, productivity will increase, and you will no longer be a slave to your law firm. Your practice will grow with ease, and you will be free to choose the type of law firm—and life—you want.

Many lawyers want to be just that: a lawyer. Owning a

business is not their life's goal, but simply a path to the courtroom. If this is you, then building a firm that essentially runs itself will create more time for you to actually practice law. A successful, autonomous firm is possible when you focus on culture first. Then, if you dream of getting back into the courtroom, you can. If you want to spend twenty days a month on the golf course, you can do so without the unrelenting ping of emails every time you tee off. I want to spend my life building a business that benefits every one of its stakeholders, so I spend my time growing our firm, improving its culture, and expanding its positive reach into our community. My partner loves practicing law, so he gets to practice law. When your law firm has a great culture, you get to choose what your relationship with the business looks like.

My mission includes helping the larger law community emulate our success. It's why I speak on stage at events. It's why I spent the last two weeks, and more than three months this year, on a beach in Costa Rica working on this book. Of course, sand and sun are not prerequisites for writing; my law firm gives me the freedom to focus on my mission and to choose to do so in a beautiful location.

In those two weeks at the beach, I had ten emails from work and no phone calls. Literally no calls. This isn't an abnormality. Two years ago, when I first went to Costa Rica for an extended vacation, I didn't hear from anyone at the office. After wondering if they were still there, I called in and asked how everyone was. They told me all was okay. They were just working away.

THE LONG JOURNEY

It was a long road to the beach in Costa Rica. Like most lawyers, I had a strong sense of justice instilled in me from a young age. I grew up in a conservative Jewish family. It was the '70s, and the Holocaust was still at the forefront of every Jewish family's mind. As a kid, I spent holidays sitting around the dinner table listening—and later participating in—family debates on government and justice. Naturally, this led to law school.

Somewhere along the line, my fascination with power shifted from the political scene to Hollywood, Wall Street, and the world of sports. I admired the high-flying moguls of sports franchises and the entertainment industry. I was fascinated with the way they rose above the regular and pushed to new levels of human achievement. After graduating law school, I set my sights on becoming a movie agent, producer, and eventually studio chief.

It only took a few years of Hollywood disillusionment to send me back to San Francisco, where a friend introduced me to the lawyer running the Tupac Shakur estate. Many people still consider Tupac the greatest rapper of all time, and I spent close to eighteen years working with his estate. I represented other high-profile rappers, many of whom were deceased. Unfortunately, those guys die at a fast clip. My more-alive client roster grew to include first-round NFL and NBA draft picks, Olympic athletes, a world champion boxer, filmmakers, comedians, the founder of Myspace, one of the more successful entrepreneurs to come out of *Shark Tank*, and even a guy who attempted to jump off Mount Everest in a wingsuit on live television.

It was sports and entertainment law at the highest level. I enjoyed working with incredibly creative people at the top of their game. Even so, I was constantly chasing the next client so I could pay the bills. I mailed out invoices that were repeatedly ignored; a football player once told me he'd never been to his mailbox. He didn't even know where it was. So, despite serving wealthy clients, I was still chasing the almighty dollar. I took on more work than I could handle and agreed to cases I wasn't excited about. I made hiring decisions I didn't love and found I never wanted to be in the office. I didn't like my firm. I was generally in a bad mood, and those around me knew it.

I traveled close to 200 days a year and was in Buffalo, New York, on a case for an NFL player, when my body decided enough was enough. On the second day of mediation, I got up from the table, felt a terrible shock to my lower back, and couldn't walk. I couldn't move. The pain was beyond incredible. My left leg was numb, and I was completely immobile. I was taken by ambulance to Buffalo General Hospital, where one of the Buffalo Bills' spine surgeons pumped me with Dilaudid, a powerful painkiller, and declared I'd ruptured a disc in my back. I needed emergency surgery.

At the time, I was representing the estate of Eazy-E, the godfather of gangster rap, in a rights infringement case. As I lay in excruciating pain, unable to move, crippled and awaiting surgery, my cell phone kept ringing. I finally answered. It was my assistant who said opposing counsel for the Eazy-E case was on the line, demanding to speak with me. Hopped up on painkillers and barely able to speak, I told my assistant to put her through.

Counsel demanded I immediately set a date for mediation or she'd file suit against my client that day. I tried to garner some sympathy, explaining I was about to be wheeled down to the operating room and didn't know how long my recovery would knock me out of the game. She didn't care. I finally asked my assistant to find a date six months out and hung up. I was reeling. I felt held hostage to these clients, their cases, and the crazy game I was playing in. My life clearly didn't belong to me. Something had to change.

DEEP LEARNING

After the surgery and three weeks stuck in a rehabilitation clinic, I hauled the remnants of my body back to San Francisco. By then, I'd been in sports and entertainment law for more than fifteen years. It was time for something new. I wanted a firm that would be more manageable, where I wouldn't have to travel so much or chase clients for hourly fees. After several years of trying to make a switch, I started taking workers' compensation cases for retired professional athletes, but found those people just as demanding as my previous clients. Eventually, I moved into broad-based consumer workers' compensation. I partnered with Bilal Kassem, a young, savvy lawyer, to finally create a firm conducive to a better lifestyle—for myself and the employees. We got intentional about serving our community and creating a fulfilling workplace.

The new focus seemed popular; we had solid marketing and received a huge number of calls. However, only about half of all inquiries resulted in a signed retainer agreement. Each lost lead was worth thousands in fees. We had to increase our conversion rate—a term I didn't really understand at the time. I started reading business books and attending seminars, through which I learned that revising our intake process alone wouldn't be enough to build the workplace we envisioned. Every part of the firm must act like a real business. The whole thing had to change, and it would require more than adopting good marketing and sales strategies.

This began a seven-year period of deep learning. I read books by legendary business minds and studied works by the ancient stoic philosophers. I became a student of human nature. I patchworked together ideas from the likes of Simon Sinek, Chip Conley, Daniel Coyle, Jim Collins, Daniel Pink, Ryan Holiday, Brené Brown, and many others I'll quote within these pages. The teachings of these masters meshed together and built upon each other in my mind. My research led me to the subject of company culture, which intrigued me. My partner, Bilal, and I implemented many ideas to improve our firm's culture. Some worked tremendously well; others failed miserably. We course-corrected and continued learning—as we continue to do to this day. The beauty was and is that we grew faster and stronger than I could have ever imagined.

A NEW ATTITUDE

We now have almost fifty employees in two offices. We've grown our revenue by more than 1,300 percent over five years. Our last in-house survey showed that every single responding employee is "happy" or "very happy" at work. We throw more than fifty social events a year and can now afford to be pillars of our community, supporting programs for the homeless and other local causes.

We were nominated for *Inc.* magazine's Best Workplaces in America, and we were named one of the fastest-growing law firms in America on three occasions. We have twice been named to the Inc. 5000 list of fastest-growing companies in America, which considers *all* industries, and we even made the Bay Area 100—a rundown of the San Francisco Bay Area's fastest-growing companies. More importantly, my phone doesn't ring off the fucking hook anymore. Bilal and I are far more fulfilled by our work, and so are our team members. Some have won our company's Hero Award for incredible achievements, like securing free rent for a year for a struggling client and getting another client and her children into a domestic violence shelter. We have a mission and we care for our people.

Reconnecting with a long-lost mission requires more than blindly following a list of action steps. You could pick up a guide to improving corporate culture, faithfully enact each policy, and still end up with a flat and uninspired culture. When you take action without truly shifting your attitude—your *thinking*—you remain trapped. Profits stagnate and little improves for you or your stakeholders. Change must be authentic.

This book isn't just a series of action steps, although you will get ideas for action. It also abstains from surface-level gimmicks like installing a foosball table in the office. Rather, it offers a true challenge to approach your firm with a culture-first and culture-for-all attitude. It's a mindset shift that will stop you feeling like a slave to your law firm, help grow your practice, and empower you to be happy living the life you choose.

What is a culture-first and culture-for-all attitude? Let's get into it.

CHAPTER ONE

CULTURE IS HUMAN

*"One cannot hire a hand. A whole
man always comes with it."*
—PETER F. DRUCKER

When Sergio joined our firm as an assistant, he'd only recently immigrated to the United States from Colombia. He brought with him a joy for life, a big heart, and enthusiasm for our company culture, arranging one of our after-work gatherings at his favorite gay bar. He was with us for about eight months when he returned to Colombia to visit his family. He came back from his trip more despondent than I'd ever seen him. His father had late-stage cancer and was deteriorating fast. Thinking this was the end, Sergio got back on a plane and went to say goodbye. However, his dad held on. After two weeks of watching and waiting at his father's bedside, Sergio thought his dad had stabilized and decided it was safe to return to the States. As soon as he landed back on American soil, his dad passed away.

It was terrible. Sergio, of course, wanted to help his mom with the funeral arrangements and her grief. He'd been out of the office for a month and exceeded his accrued vacation days and bereavement leave, but he asked for more time off to go back to Colombia. With his family in flux, he was unsure how long he'd need.

FITTING THE CRISIS INTO THE VISION

This came at a terrible time for our young firm. We were far from our current level of success and running a lean company. We didn't have extra cash or personnel to cover another absence. My partner, Bilal; Irving, our first employee who is now our director of operations; and I sat down and talked it through.

When we started the firm, we deliberately set out to put culture first and create a positive environment for all our employees, not just the attorneys. I had known Bilal for about thirty-three seconds before sensing he was someone I could do this with. It didn't take much longer to learn that he truly shared my vision of a firm that treated humans with empathy and respect.

That first meeting was in an elevator at the Oakland workers' compensation court. I jumped in on the first floor and found myself standing next to a well-dressed young guy sporting a huge beard. The workers' comp board isn't known for its snappy dressers, so this guy stood out. He was young—late twenties, I guessed—and friendly.

"What are you here for?" he asked.

"Oh, I'm representing an athlete in a workers' comp case," I said.

We chatted for three floors before Bilal got out of the elevator. As he left, he turned around, jammed his foot in front of the closing doors, and handed me his business card. "I've always wanted to do those types of cases. If you're ever looking for help, call me." With that, he walked away.

I got back to my office, propped his card right beneath my computer screen, and left it there for months. I saw it every time I sat down to work, yet I had no reason to call. More time passed, and I got closer to starting a firm that would serve the general workers of the community instead of athletes. I decided to call the elevator guy. I sensed something good in him, and I would need good help in this new venture.

Over four months, we met regularly for dinner. We discussed the type of firm we envisioned owning and the work we wanted to do. We both wanted a successful firm that made an impact in the community, and we thought carefully about how to divide the obligations of such a firm. I would run marketing and the business, and he would manage the litigation. Our interests were complementary, and we went to great efforts to plan accordingly. He could actively manage the caseload, leaving me free to run the business side of the firm.

More critical than logistics, though, was our shared desire to create something different from our previous workplace experiences. Bilal was coming from a firm that didn't value its employees, and I was certainly on the road to burnout. I had been running in place for years and craved something new. We both wanted to create a great place to work—for ourselves and everyone around us. We dreamed of a firm with a positive culture that fulfilled all its employees. We really had no definition of that and no plan to get there. I did, however, expect I'd need to partner with good people and treat them well. That was all I knew. It was my starting point. My initial evaluation proved correct: Bilal was a good guy, so on July 14, 2014, we came together to launch Pacific Workers' Compensation Law Center. When we started the firm, I took no salary. I lived off savings. Bilal took a 50 percent pay cut from his previous job, and we poured everything we could into the business. Sergio was in the second wave of employees that came into the firm, and soon after that, he lost his father.

As Bilal and I discussed holding Sergio's job for an unknown period of time, we returned to our vision for the firm. If we were to live into our values, it shouldn't matter that Sergio was an assistant case manager, or that he was relatively new to our organization. Culture-for-all contains no caveats. It means creating a positive workplace for every member of the staff, regardless of their service history or seniority. In the early days, we'd decided empathy would be one of our core values. Now, as the shit hit the fan with a high client load and not enough staff, would we tell Sergio he couldn't go and comfort his grieving mother? No. We decided to lean in, live our values, and act with empathy.

This was a turning point for me. Before Sergio approached us with his situation, I might have considered a month-long leave for one of our lawyers or an early team member who had proven their loyalty over time. Sergio was different. He wasn't disloyal by any means, but he wasn't an original—or senior—employee. I wanted to act with empathy, but I was entrenched in decades-old lessons of how the workplace "should" operate. It took several people on our staff to guide me through this decision. With their help, I finally realized what we should do.

We offered Sergio unlimited leave to return to Colombia. He was to take as much time as he needed, and those of us left in the office would bind together and make it work. Even after acknowledging this was the right thing to do, I found it very hard. I'm the guy who never stops working, so it felt unnatural to me that anyone could ditch work for an unknown period. I wasn't comfortable with this offer, yet it felt like the only option that aligned with our values, so we pushed ahead and gave Sergio time and space to focus on his family.

In the end, he was gone for at least forty-five days within a two-and-a-half-month period. He made himself available via phone and email, and the staff covered his responsibilities. Our team was strong; they were willing to chip in and figure it out. They sacrificed time and energy to fill the gap left in Sergio's absence. They stepped up and ensured he was covered. If there's a dog pulling a sled whose paw is hurt, the rest of the pack fill in until the paw recovers. That's what we did. Our service didn't falter, and we continued to provide clients with the same high-value experience. When Sergio returned to the office, he was grateful for the support and ready to refocus on work. As time went on, he was more than happy to cover his teammates when they needed support.

We've had multiple staff members struggle through tough times. An attorney badly broke her ankle and was home for five weeks. She couldn't drive. She couldn't make court appearances. An intake specialist required emergency surgery when she had no sick days or vacation time left. Her colleagues donated their paid vacation to her. Another attorney went through a difficult medical issue and needed more than eight months off work to heal. When she eventually returned, she was so grateful for the firm's support that she dug into her work and became one of our top performers. On every occasion, we closed the gap and made it work. The employees in question returned more loyal to and engaged with the company and its mission. They developed stronger bonds with the teammates who stepped up to cover them.

We care for our colleagues and instill in them a desire to care for each other. Seeing them step up for their teammates is heartwarming. It creates a stronger company with more loyal and dedicated employees. When the challenges of life, death, injury, and heartache stand in the way of work, our reaction to them becomes the path to more prosperous work.

THE WHOLE HUMAN

A big part of our company's culture is about a humanistic approach to business. It's concerned with how you acknowledge—or ignore—that a whole human shows up to the office. We do not, cannot, hire a tiny part of an individual capable of executing commands in isolation, so a great culture *welcomes* the whole human. It doesn't pretend that a man grieving his father's death can show up at the office days later and deliver his best work. Of course he can't. Part of him is lost in suffering.

The old saying that you should leave your personal life at the door is just ridiculous. Business is personal. In fact, what is more personal than the work you commit yourself to every day? In business, we must embrace the whole person who comes to work for us. As leaders, it's our responsibility to make employees feel safe enough to acknowledge every part of themselves in the workplace. This is particularly difficult for lawyers. We are taught to be tough. We are also high achievers. We want to prove we can win cases and do our jobs well. We don't want to say, "Hey, Ms. Supervisor, I can't concentrate right now. I'm struggling." Of course, this isn't exclusively a lawyer thing. No one wants to admit they don't know something they should've learned long ago. People are afraid to raise their hand and ask for help. They don't want to look stupid or weak or incapable. They worry they'll get canned if their boss thinks they can't do their job.

When half the brain is battling these concerns, the whole brain cannot focus on the real work of serving clients. In a strong and safe culture, however, a person is not afraid to say, "I'm having a really hard time at home." They trust their supervisor will invite them in and offer support. Then, their struggle is not hidden in shame and secrecy, compounding their suffering, but addressed openly so solutions can be found and progress made.

There was a lawyer at our firm who, for the sake of this story, we'll call Kathy. She's been practicing for more than thirty years and is one of the brightest women I know. One day, she came into my office and said, "Eric, I need to talk to you."

"Sure," I said, and waved her in. She sat in the brown, leather barrel chair across from me, her shoulders slightly slumped, head slightly bowed. This was not the normal, energetic Kathy I was used to seeing.

"My husband's divorcing me," she said. "It's not something I want, but it's happening. And I don't feel like I'm all here today." She sighed deeply.

"I'm so sorry to hear that," I said. "You're among friends here. If you need to take some time, that's fine. But it might be better to be in the office around all of us who care about you."

"Yeah, everyone here's been great," she said.

We talked for twenty minutes about life and marriage

and work. At one point, she sat back in her chair, paused for a moment, then said, "You know, I've worked at five different law firms in my career. I've never felt like I could go to any of my old firms and admit I was going through something like this." She continued, "Most would figure a way to hold it against you down the road, so you just don't talk about it." She said we had created a different kind of law firm and she was very grateful for that.

It took us a long time to create an open and supportive environment. Kathy's comment made me realize I'd finally created a good place to work. That felt good—so much better than being the asshole boss. Kathy's honesty also helped improve our performance. We were aware that she would temporarily be distracted by divorce and heartache, so we did what we always do, rallied around her and filled in the holes. We continued to serve clients to our usual high standards. Nothing fell through the cracks. With that support, Kathy quickly returned to our standards.

Rallying around an employee who's struggling doesn't mean sending them home for the day. When Kathy told me about her divorce, I suggested she stay in the office. Most businesses would begrudgingly tell Kathy to take a few days off. That's the worst thing you can do. People in distress don't need to be isolated; they need to be surrounded by those who support and care for them. Instead of sending them home, offer to handle their meetings and tell them to plow through the mindless work. Let them find distraction in the mundane aspects that every job has. Take them for lunch. Shoulder some of their workload. Just don't let them be alone.

CULTURE-FIRST

Many of these ideas come from Simon Sinek, author of *Start with Why: How Great Leaders Inspire Everyone to Take Action* and *Leaders Eat Last: Why Some Teams Pull Together and Others Don't*. Sinek's TED Talk on the concept of "why" has over 43 million views and is subtitled in forty-eight languages. Sinek explains how to move people with heart and emotion, as these are the factors that drive decision-making. He suggests when someone is struggling, we don't ask, "Why aren't you performing?" Rather, we say, "How can we help you? Let's work this out together." His work focuses on the great things that happen when we create a culture of safety and togetherness.

You may think you shouldn't have to get together with your employees and help them work through divorces, grief, or heartache. And sure, in an ideal world, people would be able to deliver their best every day, regardless of their life circumstances. We know that's not realistic, though. Shit happens all the time. Every one of us experiences breakups, family drama, frantic schedules, arguments, excitement, life, loss, and love. It is an extraordinary challenge to deal with all these elements. It requires embracing the personal hopes and dreams, life quirks, and challenges of your employees. You are not responsible for their emotions, but you must embrace them. After all, people spend more time at work than in any other place. They must feel safe to show up whole.

A company that prioritizes culture provides a sanctuary from our crazy society. Our country has become deeply divided. In the United States today, politicians, social influencers, and the media control the wider culture. Unfortunately, our cultural thought leaders have become the Kim Kardashians of the world. Staged reality shows, however, set false standards. It feels like our culture is now in a constant decline to the lowest common denominators. Everywhere we look there is lying, misdeed, and misdirection. We live in a culture of tainted values and deception.

In addition to politics and pop culture, regional norms also influence us. In San Francisco's Bay Area, where we are based, one out of every 11,000 people is a billionaire. It's a place where the get-rich-quick mentality thrives. We're home to countless tech companies in which owners are driven to build, get financed, get big, and exit fast. There's far more focus on venture money and round valuations than on actual product and service.

Thankfully, corporate cultures need not be tied to societal or regional norms. When a company puts its culture first, when it has principles and is principled, when it has values that it speaks to, lives by, and leans into, it becomes a safe haven from the declining culture around us. It rises above deception, getting big, exiting fast, and all the other pitfalls of our wider environment. People can leave the cultural crap of the world at the office door. They can walk into work and find the satisfaction they crave within the company walls. They feel cared for. They understand they are part of something larger than themselves. They know their company is a place of higher standards—somewhere that worries about them, their hopes, and their dreams. It becomes a staggering contrast to the lying, deception, and decline in the outside world.

CULTURE-FOR-ALL

Culture must come first for everybody, not only for the attorneys in your firm. Our industry has a habit of ignoring support staff—paralegals, assistants, receptionists, IT techs, the mailroom staff, operations teams—making them feel like second-class citizens. In almost every law firm I've encountered, these employees have an inherent feeling that their professional development does not matter, as they are not on track to become lawyers. I am certain this problem is rampant amongst all professional service organizations, but law firms feel it particularly acutely.

I was on an airplane a few years ago and got to chatting with the guy sitting next to me. He was also a lawyer running his own firm. "How many people do you have?" I asked.

"There's four of us," he said.

"So, two attorneys and two paralegals?" I said.

"Oh, no, I mean four lawyers. We have five assistants, so I guess there's nine in total. But we have four lawyers," he said.

This guy forgot more than half his workforce. He was very successful in an interesting practice, and I'm guessing they work their asses off for him, yet he essentially ignored their existence. Unfortunately, he's not alone in this. It's common for law firms to consider attorneys first and other employees second—if at all.

Many years ago, I visited a law office in Atlanta. When I arrived at the downtown, high-rise building, the receptionist welcomed me into the office. It was a well-appointed space, with lots of beautiful, dark wood furniture and bookshelves filled with mementos.

"Good morning, Mr. Farber," she said, and offered to take my coat.

"I'm sorry, just call me Eric," I said. "When you say, 'Mr. Farber,' I'm looking for my father."

She laughed and showed me through to a conference room. I was partnering with them on a case for an NFL player and was to spend the week working out of their office taking depositions. As the first day wore on, the non-attorneys continued to address me as Mr. Farber. Every time, I asked that they call me Eric instead. I noticed everyone addressed the attorneys as Mr. or Ms. but used first names for support staff.

On the second day, one of the attorneys took me aside and requested that I ensure all support staff addressed me by my last name. I respected their request but was shocked by the whole thing. They insisted that attorneys be shown a level of deference that was deliberately withheld from support staff. It created a culture of hierarchy—a caste system that labeled support staff as less deserving of respect than attorneys.

I guess policies like these are borne from outdated tradition and some sort of respect for "profession," but they reinforce the myth that support staff are second-class citizens. There is certainly some value in respecting tradition, but it does not outweigh the need to create a great environment for every employee. When support staff feel like second-class citizens, they do not feel safe or secure in their position. They don't assume they have the ability to grow. They are barely in their seat—kind of doing their work while probably looking for another job.

In addition to demoralizing support staff, the caste system puts undue pressure on attorneys. They feel the weight of carrying the firm and constantly strive to earn the title bestowed on them. Often, that pressure is the very reason that a paralegal never sought to become a lawyer, or the receptionist doesn't set their sights higher. Lawyers are constantly under pressure—to win a case, to run a firm, to bring about justice. It starts in law school when classes become 90 percent of life. There's little space for family or anything else. Later, practicing law becomes all-consuming. It's intense. Many people are simply not interested in making work their everything. They want jobs with less responsibility. Others wanted to attend law school but couldn't afford the fees, or stayed home to care for a grandparent, or weren't confident in their academic abilities. These are not lesser people. They simply have different career goals.

I'd put the IQ of our mailroom manager up against any of our lawyers. I knew he was someone different when I went into the mailroom on his first day and found him playing jazz on the stereo. We had a conversation about 1980s music. I discovered he was more than smart. He was cultured. He was no different than any of our lawyers (or many of our other people)—except that he'd spent much of his life as a ranch hand at his uncle's acreage on the California coast. He didn't want the lawyer lifestyle. He became—and remains—an excellent employee. He's engaged. He makes sure the work is done right. Nothing gets by him because he is a professional in that mailroom, and we treat him as such.

When you have a caste system, support staff feel that they are of less value at work. They feel like supporting players who are less responsible for the success of a case or the success of the firm. At our firm, we've created a culture where support staff are equal and feel an equal responsibility to the clients. Our mailroom manager knows he plays an important role in our clients' and our firm's success.

Most professionals engage in professional development. They take classes, attend retreats, and improve themselves. The law industry's caste system extends into education. Firms support their attorneys' growth but do almost nothing to assist in the training and development of support staff. Sure, there's some training when new people come in, but few firms truly concentrate on the development of their non-lawyers so they can become masters of their job. Most people want to be great at their job. They want the recognition that comes with that, and they want to know when they screw up so they can do better.

In our firm, we've seen the greatest growth when support staff feel we care about their professional and personal development—just as much as we do for the lawyers. We now have initiatives to deliberately develop non-attorneys, including constant training courses, an online educational platform, and programs that address the whole person, such as a wellness program, community outreach, and a speaker series. Anyone can attend these programs, but they are led by non-lawyers and designed to improve the self-esteem, self-value, and fulfillment of support staff. Through these initiatives, we allow every employee to excel. We treat everyone as a first-class citizen. This pays off. When we invest in the growth of our support staff, their performance improves. Invariably, so does that of our company.

There is a balance to be found here. We knew our success would depend upon our support staff, so we focused on them intensely, ensuring they knew they were just as important as anyone else at the firm. However, we soon came to see that we were neglecting our lawyers, who had begun to feel like cogs in the machine, important yet often overlooked. In our attempt to balance the scale, we'd overcompensated. When we recognized the lawyers' discontent, we made adjustments and moved closer to a culture-for-all environment. We had taught ourselves the need to identify and fine-tune the culture of our firm at any given time, as I'll discuss in chapter three.

360-CULTURE

With growth comes increased interactions. A firm improves its efforts and is able to serve more clients, impact more lives, hire a larger staff, contract outside vendors, serve even more clients, and so on in an upward spiral. As the firm circles upwards, its sphere of influence increases. It touches the lives of more people.

A 360-culture is the idea of getting in sync with every person with whom your firm interacts. It's about joining forces with employees, clients, vendors, and a community to work towards the same vision. In a 360-culture, everyone rows the boat together. They may come from different places and have unique goals, but they pull together in the same direction. They're all heading for the same north star. This cultural collaboration enables them to move faster.

They row together internally, and they also row alongside external partners. No firm works in isolation. We inevitably interact with other law firms and vendors. Often, our success requires their cooperation. At times, we rely on their professional courtesy, such as when we need a deadline extension or paperwork expedited. You should extend your culture out to touch the firms and vendors surrounding you. One of our values is empathy, and we do not just reserve this for fellow team members. We treat other firms and vendors with empathy and, in doing so, we earn their respect. They simply like us more. They're willing to go above and beyond for us, and that can be of enormous benefit in difficult cases.

In chapter eight, we'll discuss extending your culture into marketing to prospective clients. For now, know that you can use your culture to better connect with colleagues, other firms, vendors, and existing clients, helping all of those relationships thrive.

Company culture means acknowledging the whole human who arrives in the office. By extension, staff must see our clients as real people, not just case numbers. In a high-volume shop such as ours, it's particularly important to attach some humanity to the person on the end of the phone. Without it, staff can easily slip into short phone calls, short tempers, and an attitude of annoyance toward the very people who are paying the bills.

To see our clients as full people, we encourage our intake specialists to gather as much information as possible about a client's family, kids, grandkids, pets, hobbies, and so on during the onboarding process. The basic facts about the person and their injury are just the skeleton; the information about them as people begins to attach flesh to those bones. Then they ask for a photograph of the client, which puts a true human face to the client. They pass this person to the team who assigned that case. When the team sees a client as an actual human with a family, dreams, and ambitions, they work harder on the client's behalf. They form relationships with the client, and this builds trust. When concerned, dedicated, well-trained staff build their own relationships with the clients, this relieves the pressure from attorneys to field all the client calls.

We're still developing and refining our process here, but we've seen even small steps towards humanizing clients make a difference. Trust building has been one of the biggest factors in improving the quality of life for our attorneys. When clients trust their case manager and assistant case manager, they don't feel they must hear from their lawyer as often. Support staff can take client calls, manage information, and fulfill the client's need to be heard. In so many law firms, support staff simply file documents and take messages for the lawyers, but it is impossible for the lawyers to call everyone back. Building team-wide trust with clients lets us reserve our lawyers' time for important calls, court appearances, and the other tasks that only they can do. This has been one of the key components in creating an unparalleled level of customer service.

This trust doesn't just help us balance the workload between team members. Trust is vital in achieving the best client outcomes. Without trust, it's almost impossible to motivate a client to take action. They're slow to send information. They'll easily become upset with a lengthy legal process. And they'll struggle to accept bad news, such as a proposed settlement they weren't expecting. If there is no trust in the relationship, a client will not believe you when they say it's in their best interest to accept a settlement.

Daniel Pink, a former lawyer turned best-selling author on the human condition, discusses this concept in his *New York Times* best-selling book *To Sell Is Human: The Surprising Truth about Moving Others*. He tells the story of Yehonatan Turner, an Israeli radiologist and a resident at the Shaare Zedek Medical Center in Jerusalem. Radiologists have little patient interaction. They sit and review CT scans to determine what should be done for the patients. It is long, lonely work. Occasionally, in reviewing the scans, the radiologists get incidental findings—that is, they find something of note that has nothing to do with the original reason for the patient's visit. For example, a patient may have a suspected tear in the knee, and the radiologist may, while examining the knee scan, find an unrelated cyst. These incidental findings are often to thank for the early detection of serious medical issues.

With the patients' approval, Turner and his team took 300 patient photographs and attached them to the scans. They wanted to see what happened when a radiologist was reminded that a scan belonged to a real person. As the radiologists began their assessments, a photo of the respective patient would pop-up on their screen. The team recorded the radiologists' CT scan findings, those that related to the purpose of the scan and those that were incidental.

Three months later, Turner's team showed those same scans to the same group of radiologists, but this time, without the accompanying patient photographs. These radiologists review so many scans each day, with very little patient information, that they didn't realize they'd already seen these particular scans. Amazingly, they missed 80 percent of the incidental findings they'd previously identified. So, when they felt like they were dealing with real people, they were 80 percent more likely to spot incidental findings that could have a huge impact on a patient's health. Without the humanizing effect of the photographs, they missed these incidentals 80 percent of the time. Of course, Turner included a control group in the study, and it confirmed that the difference in humanized assessments was shocking.

Studies like this illustrate the need to turn clients into humans. In any high-volume practice, we can unintentionally anonymize our clients. Seeing details of a client's background, understanding them as a person with parents and children, living a life full of hopes and wishes just like everyone else, we can start to build empathy for the client. Team members can create stronger bonds with the client and ultimately try to achieve better results for them. We're still refining our process here, but it has already been a game-changer for us. Our empathy and drive to do well for the clients is increasing with every step along this path. In turn, we have seen our average case value increase.

In addition to looking at our clients as whole humans, we seek to be *considered* whole humans by our vendors. Just as our clients need to trust us, we need to trust those we do business with. That's why we interview vendors with the same vigor we use when interviewing prospective employees, as we'll discuss in more depth later on. We assess potential vendors for their soft skills, culture, and ability to grow. We want to work with companies comprised of good people, good processes, and good growth. This ensures they will care about us as a client. It means things will get done, and they will continue to get things done as we grow in the future.

A REASON TO WORK

Culture-for-all allows every employee to feel part of a mission, a movement, a purpose. Our mission has grown and shifted over time and will probably continue to do so. Our principles document states maxims such as "Always tell the truth," and "Fail well—together and individually," which never change. Our stated mission and values, some of which are based on these principles, *can* evolve as priorities and goals shift. As I write, our mission is to be the industry leader in plaintiffs' workers' compensation law by providing world-class service to our clients, our team, and our community. This is inspired by our ever-solid principles of high-quality work, service, and community. People may get used to the idea that they'll sit in a cubicle for the rest of their lives, but they really want to be part of something bigger than themselves. They want to know their work efforts aren't wasted. Our mission provides our staff with a real reason to come to work every day. They are part of a company that is changing an industry, and they know they are part of that change.

When researching this book, I did a completely unscientific study of my own. I reached out to many attorneys I know who run their own firms and asked them three questions:

1. Do you have a stated company mission?
2. Do you have stated company values?
3. What role does culture play in your firm?

None of the leaders I spoke with had a mission statement they shared with their team. Only one had stated company values that they shared with their team. All of them said culture was important, but none could really define their culture.

It is kind to offer your employees the opportunity to pursue a meaningful mission, and it is also a smart business move. The greatest companies in the world operate around a mission in which all their employees are engaged. Take Coca-Cola, for example. They sell sugar water, yet are on a self-declared mission to:

1. Refresh the world
2. Inspire moments of optimism and happiness
3. Create value and make a difference

Consumers know it as simply "making people feel happy." They understand this from the company's marketing, which includes slogans such as "Open Happiness" and "Taste the Feeling." Many of us still remember the famous Coke commercial in which a little boy hands a Coke to a despondent and hobbling Mean Joe Greene in the stadium tunnel after coming off the field injured during a game, or their 1971 "Hilltop" commercial with the jingle, "I want to buy the world a Coke, and keep it company." It was so famous and impactful that the multi-award-winning television drama *Mad Men* used the actual commercial as the final scene in its series finale. These true messages of mission are what move people and, in turn, build lasting impressions.

Most lawyers, deep down, are mission-driven. They entered the industry because they felt drawn to deliver justice. This is an easier mission to inspire than that of selling sugar water, or ensuring a package is delivered within eight hours, or serving the best greasy diner food around. A law firm's *beauty* is in its mission. It's attractive and should be an easy idea to sell to non-attorneys. We can say, "Join us and make the world a better place. Help us fight for justice."

Whether or not your mission is stated on paper, you already know it. It's why you went to law school, and it's why you started your firm in the first place. If you haven't written it down and shared it with your team, it is time to do so. Then, talk openly about it. Include it in your job ads, your website, and your social media. It's why you exist, so there is no shame in sharing this.

CULTURE IS DISCIPLINE

People don't often talk about mission, and they certainly don't talk much about discipline—at least, not in a positive way. When most people consider discipline, they think of disciplinarians. They imagine an army sergeant shouting and punishing people for wrongdoings. However, being disciplined is different from being a disciplinarian. Discipline is simply the ability to monitor yourself. It means that when you commit to waking up at

6 a.m. to get to work on time, you follow through, because *discipline directs action.*

In his book *Good to Great: Why Some Companies Make the Leap...and Others Don't,* Jim Collins, the intellectual heir of Peter Drucker, spends a great deal of time explaining the role of discipline in great companies. He says, "A culture of discipline is not a principle of business; it's a principle of greatness." He noted that the key to greatness is disciplined people making disciplined decisions, which they implement through disciplined action. That means executing procedures and processes the same way each time. It's having a strategic system for everything, whether it's hiring new staff, compiling a case, or even opening the mail. It's documenting these systems, training staff in them, and measuring their results.

In our firm, we spend a great deal of time working on processes, constantly tweaking and refining them. A business is, after all, just a series of interlocking systems. We try to map out these systems and processes to continually improve them. Even our processes have processes. I am not being facetious here. One process we are consistently refining is that for developing other processes. This includes making certain that changes are communicated and rolled out effectively. Recently, a law passed in California requiring sexual harassment training. It is rare that we have training courses that everyone is required to take, with a deadline attached. This gave us the opportunity to really review how we communicated the new training to everyone. We improved our communication process and now apply that to other areas of our business.

We'll talk in-depth about hiring processes in chapter seven. For now, I want you to understand that disciplined processes differ from micromanaging. As Jocko Willink, former Navy SEAL and author of *Extreme Ownership*, says, "Be disciplined to be free." Disciplined processes free employees to focus on the more complex and fulfilling aspects of their work. Micromanaging involves constantly watching people and preventing them from being their true selves. Micromanaging keeps such a tight leash on employees that they cannot fail. That may sound attractive, but without failure, there is no growth, and fewer opportunities to develop trust, as we discussed earlier.

When you create a disciplined environment, you teach employees that you care about the realities of coming to work every day. They understand that you have implemented processes to handle the mundane, so they can focus on fulfilling work. Then, they understand the idea that the work is important and worthy of their full attention.

The final value in discipline is that it balances a culture of fun. When there is fun without discipline, nothing gets done. As discipline directs action, it ensures shit still gets done, even when you're having fun. It prevents you from creating a place where employees hang out around the office foosball table eating the free lunches while the firm goes under because the employees are too busy playing fucking foosball to do any real work. If you want a culture of fun, you need a culture of discipline. One balances the other.

John Berry Jr. offers a great example of the benefits of discipline in a law firm. He's the managing attorney of the Berry Law Firm, a practice specializing in criminal and national veterans' law in Nebraska. Berry is tall and almost imposing. He dresses impeccably well and is in great shape. A former US Army Ranger, he has clearly stuck with his morning military workouts. Berry Law Firm was founded by his father, John Berry Sr. who is a legendary trial lawyer in Nebraska. Berry Jr. joined the firm in 1994 after spending time in the military and then attending law school. I recently had the opportunity to speak with him about the success of the firm, which he attributes to a military-style culture.

He told me that when he joined the firm, there were eight people there, and it was a difficult place for him to work. Although his father was a great trial lawyer, he did not have the same aptitude for running a growing practice. The office was chaotic and disorganized. People worked hard at the firm, but the cases came inconsistently, and the firm fluctuated in a feast-and-famine cycle. After just eighteen months working there, Berry Jr. was, as he puts it, "happily deployed back to Iraq." He returned in 2006 to discover little had changed. His father's office was still chaotic. Over nine long years working there, he tried over fifty jury trials and was still in the National Guard. The work was intense, and the staff were just not developing in a way that they could help. The pressure began to destroy his family.

Berry Jr. began to think about the times he was happiest at work. They were all when he was in the US Army's infantry, leading teams of 140 soldiers. He thought about the systems, processes, chain of command, and people who executed missions in the infantry and made his time there so satisfying. He wondered if he could apply some of those elements to his father's firm. In the meantime, he was eager to grow the practice. He tried many things, even hiring two of the better-known law firm consulting companies to help—at the same time. At the end of the day, though, he came to the conclusion that a bit of military style was required. That meant having the right people and the right processes. He took the leap and fired someone who definitely was not right. She was an assistant who was great at her work but who had a toxic attitude. She would yell at others in the office, and that just wasn't what Berry Jr. wanted. When he finally fired her, others in the office took note. They saw Berry Jr. was serious about improving the environment, and yelling wouldn't fly anymore.

Berry Jr. and the team began creating more systems and chains of command. They defined their mission: to serve 100,000 veterans. They focused on a culture of discipline inspired by the military. Things started to change. More work came in. The firm grew, and the culture became far more enjoyable. Berry Jr. knew things were working well when an attorney came to him to say her husband's job had been relocated, and they had to move to Australia for a year, but she didn't want to leave the firm. She wanted to remain a part of what they'd created there. They agreed for her to work remotely for that year, and the arrangement worked well. Since 2015, when Berry Jr. started focusing on military-style discipline, the Berry Law Firm has grown from about eight people to over sixty, and their revenue has soared from just over $3 million to over $7.5 million in 2018.

CULTURE IS AIR

A disciplined company culture provides a purpose that fulfills an individual beyond a paycheck. Culture is a mission that engages a person's humanity and motivates them to action. In turn, it becomes the air a company breathes, giving life and enabling growth. Ignoring the mission in the work and the humanity of the employees leads to frustration and stagnation. A good culture welcomes the whole human into the mission, does it in a disciplined manner, and does it for everyone, regardless of position or tenure. This breathes life into a business. It's not about being nice and creating kumbaya moments for other people; when employees feel fulfilled, productivity soars.

When Sergio asked for indefinite leave to return to Colombia and comfort his mother, he was a relatively new, junior employee. Before that terrible time, we knew Sergio was a good guy. Since then, he has continued to prove himself a loyal, conscientious, and hard worker. Had we behaved like most firms, he likely would have quit after we declined him leave, or stayed and been resentful, before eventually leaving anyway. Thankfully, we lived into our values of empathy and humanity, and remained patient as Sergio spent time with his family. He rewarded us with more loyalty, enthusiasm, and conscientious work than we ever could've hoped for. Sergio serves us and our clients incredibly well, as does the rest of our team.

Embracing the humanity in your workforce is incredibly rewarding, but also overwhelming. When you're willing to interact with the whole range of human experiences for yourself and your employees, it can feel like opening the floodgates. Plato said, "The part can never be well unless the whole is well." To bring wellness to your employees, and therefore your firm, you must attend to the health of the parts of people that you might not ordinarily interact with. This might leave you bombarded with emotions and egos, personality quirks and strange circumstances. You'll start to see how needy humans can be, and that's what we'll look at next.

CHAPTER TWO

HUMAN NEEDS AT WORK

"If you pay peanuts, you get monkeys."
—CHINESE PROVERB

There once was a lawyer who died and found himself standing at the pearly gates of heaven. St. Peter was there to greet him, dressed in long robes and radiating light. The angel opened his arms wide and announced to the lawyer, "You can choose to spend eternity here in heaven or down in hell. To help you decide, you get to test each place out. Where would you like to start?"

"I'll try heaven first," said the lawyer, so St. Peter cranked open the pearly gates and ushered him in. The lawyer spent the morning sitting around on a cloud, playing the harp, and being angelic. It was boring as hell. Then he went down to test the real hell and found a raging party. There were Jell-O shots and drinking games, and Bon Jovi music blasted from a stage surrounded by lava.

The lawyer went back to St. Peter and said, "Well, this sounds crazy, but I choose hell. It's a lot more fun." St. Peter sighed and sent him back down. But when the lawyer returned, the party was over. A demon tied him to a desk and tortured him for every minute of the long, long day. Finally, the lawyer spoke up. "What's going on?" he asked. "I came here before and it was so much fun. But this...?"

The demon nodded. "Yeah, that was our summer associate program. This is the real thing."

WHEN THE PROMISE DOESN'T MATCH THE REALITY

Before starting law school, I clerked at a big firm based in Phoenix, Arizona. It was a great experience. The firm was an early leader in the tech industry, representing both Microsoft and Apple at the time. During my first year of law school, they invited me to return to Phoenix and join their summer associate program. The pay would have covered my law school tuition for at least the next year. I also heard rumors that the program included two weeks in a luxury condo in Hawaii, long lunches with a different lawyer every day, and the best tickets to sporting events.

I declined. Instead, I opted for an unpaid internship at the public defender's office. My father was not pleased.

Although the pay and bonuses were tempting, I'd always felt like a bit of an outsider and I wasn't sure a big firm was right for me. I didn't feel right accepting the summer associate position when I wasn't interested in working there after law school. Many of my classmates, however, attended similar summer associate programs. They were wined and dined and shown the great lifestyle that would be theirs if they worked for whoever was courting them. This still happens. I'm sure you've seen it. Firms woo young associates and hire them from other firms or straight out of school. They promise, "This is an amazing place. When you sit at this desk, you become part of the family. You'll love this work. It's everything you've wanted since you were eight years old. You're going to be here forever."

When the young associate is finally hired as an attorney, he or she works long, lonely hours tied to their desk. Then the firm turns around and demands that the associate bring in their own clients. Suddenly this overworked lawyer is tasked with marketing, and they know their job is at risk if they don't bring in enough business.

We all know this isn't just a case of new-hire hazing. A friend of mine works for a mid-sized healthcare firm where the partners are playing in the seven- and sometimes eight-figure annual generations. My friend was doing about $3 million of business a year for the firm. Another partner there was having a bad year. He'd brought in less than expected—a million dollars less. I remember a conversation with my friend in which he wondered how long the firm would let this long-time partner continue at a lower rate of generations. Within a few months, they'd canned him. He'd been there for more than fifteen years. My friend was shocked. This happened years ago, but it always stuck with me. There's just no heart in that type of weeding out. Sure, a law firm can't afford to take a hit of a million dollars a year, or consistently support an underperforming employee. How, though, can we expect attorneys to perform their best when they're under constant fear of being fired? That is a broken culture.

Smaller firms don't generally offer summer internship programs, but they do offer their own promises to prospective hires. They say, "Hey, we're nice people. We have benefits. We care about our employees. Want to come work for us?" The interviewee says, "Sure," but when they rock up, they discover the firm isn't everything they were promised. They don't care for their employees in real, tangible ways. They might have some interesting initiatives, but they ignore the most basic human needs of their staff.

Basic human needs, such as safety, discipline, trust, and society, have always existed, but traditional workplace cultures ignore them to their detriment. As I said before, it is the job of a leader to care for their employees. In turn, employees will care for the clients, and the clients will care for everybody.

Caring for employees means meeting, and then going far beyond, their basic human needs. This provides them with a high degree of safety and security. They can then feel safe to shift their focus to higher problem-solving and service. Staff who feel cared for are free to work harder for your firm. They thrive as individuals, and in turn, create a thriving company. They won't leave for another firm. When you provide for and then exceed their basic needs, care for them, and create a safe place to develop as professionals, they become your biggest fans. They become un-poachable. No other employer will be able to steal them. They will love where they work and want to remain by your side.

BASIC HUMAN NEEDS—AND BEYOND

So, what are the basic human needs that you must meet and exceed? Most people learned about this by studying Maslow's hierarchy of needs in school. This is a theory developed by psychologist Abraham Maslow in the mid-twentieth century. His theory says that people have common motivations for their actions, and as each motivation is fulfilled, they move up the pyramid to focus on a higher motivation. The kicker is that each tier of the pyramid must be satisfied before they can move upwards.

At the base of the pyramid are physiological needs, such as food, shelter, and warmth. The second tier is safety, which involves personal, emotional, and financial security, health and well-being. The next level up is love and belonging. This is about feeling accepted in a social or family group. The penultimate tier is esteem, which relates to getting recognition and respect from others and for oneself. At the top of the pyramid is self-actualization—achieving one's full potential. There's a lot of theory behind these ideas, and I'm not a psychologist. Thankfully, I was able to learn from two incredible authors who distilled these ideas into something I could apply to a law firm.

In the early days of our firm when we were still struggling, I was reading an enormous number of books to try and find solutions to so many of the issues around a quickly growing practice, one of which was a profound level of turnover—over 70 percent annually. I found John Morgan, one of the big guys in the legal profession. Since 1988, Morgan's firm has grown from one office in Florida to over 500 lawyers in more than forty offices in thirteen states, boasting over $5 billion in settlements. He wrote the seminal book on growing a practice, *You Can't Teach Hungry: Creating the Multimillion Dollar Law Firm.* In it, he says, "If people are leaving, you're either not paying enough, or you're a jerk." I tried the not-jerk option first, as I didn't believe we had the cash to pay enough. Not being a jerk was the cheaper choice, and it aligned with my goal to be a better boss. We had some success, but our turnover was still very high.

One weekend, after losing a key employee to better pay in another company, I woke up early and sat down to work on changing our incentive programs so we could better compensate our people. I really struggled to figure this out. As our cash flow was tight, we'd created several different and incredibly complicated profit-sharing programs for the staff. I talked the issue through with my wife, Diana, and she reminded me that the staff are not entrepreneurs. If they wanted the risk of starting a business, they'd be working for themselves. Instead, they wanted to be sure we'd take care of them enough that they wouldn't have to live paycheck to paycheck. She recommended I read Chip Conley's book *Peak: How Great Companies Get Their Mojo from Maslow.* I did, and it persuaded me to finally get on board with paying more, not just offering more performance incentives. Conley is a *New York Times* best-selling author, the founder and former CEO of Joie de Vivre Hospitality (the second-largest operator of boutique hotels in the US), and a strategic advisor for Airbnb—the business that revolutionized the hotel industry. He has so many accolades that it's hard to list them all, but he was notably named Most Innovative CEO by the *San Francisco Business Times*. He knows business and understands the wisdom needed for a company to become, as he puts it, "self-actualized." It starts with people.

In *Peak*, he discusses how business theory has traditionally held the idea that workers are lazy and must be tightly managed. Conley argues this isn't true, and that fulfilling a person's human needs and moving up Maslow's pyramid towards self-actualization will motivate them to the point where they don't need such intensive management. He says you must start by meeting their basic needs: a decent wage, insurance, clothes, food, and shelter. Most companies don't even pay enough to cover these things anymore. The poor are getting poorer, and administrative assistants and frontline employees are getting squeezed out of housing markets. Spot bonuses and a chance at profit sharing simply aren't sufficient to make them feel safe. They are not the risk-taking business owner you are. They want a guarantee that working for you will provide them with a decent living, so they can take care of themselves and their family. Free lunches are nice, but they don't matter if the admin assistant is sitting there thinking, *I can't pay my fucking rent this month.*

This book was a game-changer for me. At the time, I

wasn't a jerk, but we still weren't paying much. *Peak* helped me realize that if employees are living in scarcity, worried about paying rent or buying groceries, you can't expect them to show up and deliver their best at work. We were asking our people to concentrate on complicated tasks and produce extremely high-quality work. Within days of reading the book, I started to question if it was even possible for them to deliver what we asked when we weren't giving them enough air to breathe.

PAY LIKE YOU MEAN IT!

John Morgan's quote got me thinking but Conley's book was mind-shifting. It prompted true self-assessment. I looked at how we operate, what we want from our law firm, and the legacy we're trying to create. With Conley's teaching, we flipped everything on its head. We immediately reevaluated our pay structures. We stopped the complicated incentive programs and committed to paying everyone as much as possible, with as many benefits as possible. If that meant we, the owners, had to take a lot less home, so be it. We began with the frontline jobs. We explained to our lawyers what we were doing and that, if it worked, they would also see large salary increases as we worked up the ladder. Our most junior people got immediate raises, and we rolled out pay increases to everyone else over a short period. As we grew, we increased our offerings.

To determine the salary increases, I looked at the cost of living in San Francisco's Bay Area, where we're located, for the demographic we employed. I researched what other workers' compensation firms paid these positions. Then I realized that this demographic was too narrow. I had to look beyond the workers' comp field to the wider legal marketplace where employees might be enticed to go. I began to research what general law firms paid for those positions. It quickly became clear that this wasn't good enough. Our area has one of the lowest unemployment rates in the country, and our support staff could easily get jobs in any industry. They weren't confined to law. So, I finally considered what it would take to make people *happy* with their pay rate.

Although we gave instant raises, it took several iterations to bring our pay structure to a point where it makes us and our employees happy. Four years after reading *Peak*, some positions pay double what they were before. Some roles started at thirteen dollars an hour, just above the minimum wage for our area. They now pay as much as twenty-five dollars an hour or more.

We assessed health insurance. Early on, we couldn't find the cash to immediately increase health insurance contributions, so we committed to annual increases, which gave us time to find the money. In the meantime, I went on a mission to find benefits that were out of the ordinary.

I found a program called Gradifi, which let us give small, incremental amounts each month to help staff pay back student loans. Gradifi places these company payments on the back end of these loans, significantly reducing the overall amounts owed. Gradifi was in beta at the time and only allowed a few companies to use their system. The companies they let in, however, were much bigger than our firm. I called Gradifi at least twenty-five times and begged them to let us in, even though we were tiny. They finally did, and we now offer the benefit of helping pay down employees' student loans. I took the same approach with our 401(k). We learned about America's Best 401k, which shifts retirement account costs to the employer, so the employee can save more and earn more over time. Upon learning how this worked and that it let companies shoulder the burden of the costs rather than the employees, we switched.

These out-of-the-ordinary benefits combined with raises and gradual insurance increases helped drastically reduce our turnover. People began to see we were committed to them. They started to believe that our mission was more than just corporate bullshit. We were taking action to try and make them happy. That made them want to stay.

Even when done gradually, increasing pay and benefits cost money. Initially, I believed we couldn't afford to increase pay rates, but here's what I learned: If you can't pay enough, you shouldn't be in business. You *have* to figure out how to get there. On paper, we couldn't do it. The margins in our business are very low and we didn't have space to find more money. However, we decided we would increase pay, so my partner and I delayed increasing our own salaries and sacrificed our pay for the greater good. We also committed to growth. To pay more, we *had* to grow. It was the only way to find the money we needed for meaningful pay and benefits increases. To grow, I had to learn to run a larger company. For a larger company to be successful, we needed a better culture. A better culture required improved pay structures. We had to make this a priority.

At each stage of our expansion, we forewent profit distributions. We agreed to wait six months or a year before doing another payout, so we could hire more people, promote others, and give pay raises all around. We sacrificed for our future, trusting that it would come back to us in spades. And it did. It absolutely did. We've increased our profit an insane amount. Our revenue has increased by 1,300 percent over five years. As Robert Bosch, the founder of the massive German electronics manufacturer Bosch, said, "I don't pay good wages because I've got a lot of money. I have a lot of money because I pay good wages."

Bosch made that statement in the 1880s. He was likely

one of the first businesspeople to truly understand the benefits of treating employees well. He called his staff "associates" and said they were more than just wage earners. He held company retreats and provided a form of health insurance. His was the first company in Germany to introduce an eight-hour workday. These were groundbreaking concepts at that time, and Bosch was accused of being a socialist—considered a grievous crime by many. His nickname in the German business community was Bosch the Red. His associates, however, had a different name for him: Father Bosch. This was a company in which everyone felt like family. Of course, Bosch has grown into one of the world's largest companies, grossing more than $78 billion in 2018. Father Bosch certainly understood good business.

EMOTIONAL SAFETY

Once you're paying enough to satisfy your employees' basic physiological needs, you must ensure they feel safe and secure at work. They need to feel physically safe, of course, but in a law firm, the stapler is probably the most dangerous piece of equipment they'll use. More relevant is *emotional safety*. Employees want to feel certain that their job is secure.

Most people think their job will be on the chopping block if they fail in any way. In many companies, that's true. We address this on a new employee's first day. In one of our first conversations, we explain that we expect them to fail. We're okay with it, and we don't want them to hide it. If they mess up, they should speak up. If they don't know how to do something, they're to ask for help, and their team leader will coach them through it. I'll talk more about coaching in chapter six, but telling employees you expect them to fail takes the fear out of failure. Then, they feel safe to ask questions. They're not afraid of being berated, micromanaged, disciplined, or fired.

This is a concept I learned more about in *An Everyone Culture: Becoming a Deliberately Developmental Organization* by Robert Kegan and Lisa Laskow Lahey, with Matthew L. Miller, Andy Fleming, and Deborah Helsing. As they say, "In an ordinary organization, most people are doing a second job no one is paying them for. In businesses large and small; in government agencies, schools, and hospitals; in for-profits and non-profits; and in any country in the world, most people are spending time and energy covering up their weaknesses, managing people's impressions of them, showing themselves to their best advantage, playing politics, hiding inadequacies, their uncertainties, and hiding their limitations." An organization is responsible for creating a safe environment where employees do not feel compelled to hide, but safe to address their weaknesses.

The authors of *An Everyone Culture* address this with a

new approach to business, which they refer to as a "Deliberately Developmental Organization," or DDO. In a DDO, safety and conscious development of people is at the center of the organization's ethos. The authors studied three companies which epitomize DDOs: real estate giant The Decurion Corporation, e-commerce company Next Jump, and the world's largest hedge fund, Bridgewater Capital, which was founded by Ray Dalio. These are very different businesses with two things in common; they are all intensely successful, and they all put culture first. Each employ different methods in managing their business, but their core values are common. They are devoted to their employees' development—and this is equally true for all company positions. They insist on transparency among their ranks. They create environments in which employees are challenged to create better versions of themselves. And they are consistent with all of this—which makes employees feel safe.

I had a conversation a few years ago with a lawyer who ran a firm of about forty people, ten of whom were attorneys. Back then, we had about twenty people working for us, including four or five attorneys, and we'd been in business for only a couple of years. He was impressed by our fast rate of growth and asked how we'd done it.

"We focused on creating a great work environment," I said.

He nodded. "We focus on that, too. How much business do you make your attorneys bring in?"

I immediately knew this wouldn't be a fun conversation. "I don't make them bring in any business. That's our job as the company."

He tilted his head and furrowed his brow. "I don't understand."

He didn't get it, because since the beginning of time, law firms have expected individual attorneys in the firm to be rainmakers and bring in business for the company. That's how associates get promoted to partners. If they don't bring in business over the years, they're shown the door. I took a deep breath and started my usual spiel. "I run a company. We believe it's the company's job to create an environment in which people can do great work. So, our firm does its own marketing; we bring in the business for everyone else to get done. If lawyers bring in business, that's a bonus, but it isn't required."

He was quiet, so I asked, "Do you hire new lawyers out of school?"

"Yes, of course. We do both. We hire lawyers away from other firms, and some straight out of law school."

"Let me get this straight," I said. "You go and recruit lawyers by promising them a great lifestyle, great work, and the opportunity to practice their trade and become great litigators. You say you'll pay them high wages, cover their insurance, and all the rest of it. Then they get there, and you say, 'Okay, bring in work, or you'll never make partner.' That must be scary for someone to be under pressure to both perform legal work and transform into a personal marketer. It must make for a tough environment when they think they'll be shown the door if they don't bring in enough business."

There was a long pause. "I've never really thought about that," he said.

"Well, it doesn't create a safe environment when attorneys believe their job is under threat because they can't market themselves. Law school never taught them marketing."

He asked how people were considered for partnership if they didn't bring in business. I said attorneys and support staff were assessed on how well they performed their work, how much they contributed to the company's mission, and how they kept clients happy. He seemed pretty taken aback by this idea, as are most law firm owners. I explained that the real reason we'd grown so fast was that we made our employees—all of them—feel safe, fulfilling a basic human need.

TRUST BUILDS SAFETY

Trust builds safety. When we don't trust in our environment, we don't feel safe. Trust also compels employees to work harder, leading to almost inevitable growth. One of the most renowned thought leaders on trust, vulnerability, and courage is Brené Brown, a best-selling author and researcher. I love her stuff. She says, "Trust is a product of vulnerability that grows over time and requires work, attention, and full engagement."

Allowing trust to grow over time has been difficult for me. In the early days, I expected employees to trust me immediately, yet I never trusted them. I simply wasn't a trusting person. My business naiveté compounded this problem. Back then, I ran a practice, not a business, and it didn't occur to me to study business books. As that changed and I began to learn from the best business minds, I realized trust was essential. I ran my own business; if I got sick, if my barely recovered back seized up, I would have to trust my employees to run the firm without me. I couldn't wait for the shit to hit the fan before I trusted them. I had to trust first and believe it would develop into a two-way street.

BELONGINGNESS

The first two levels of Maslow's hierarchy are about basic human needs, but to see real change in our firms, we must go above that. The third tier is about belongingness and love. In simple terms, this means people need to feel accepted in their society. People spend more time at work than anywhere else, so the human need for belongingness must be fulfilled at work. This isn't just a nice thing to do. If an employee has a best friend at work, they're far more likely to stay. You might not be able to reach self-actualization in your firm, but you must create an environment of belonging by bringing employees into the social fold. They must be welcomed into the working team, and individually invited to company events.

Today, we have more than fifty social events a year. Every Friday, we get together for twenty minutes for our Friday Wheel Spin, where we give away gifts in gratitude for excellent service. We have monthly lunches and quarterly happy hours. There's a summer barbecue, a holiday party, and a company anniversary celebration. There's impromptu stuff too. If I sense the team has lost their energy, I'll say, "Hey, let's meet at the bar after work and have a quick drink," or, "It's Sarah's birthday. Who wants to go for lunch to celebrate?"

We also have team-led social initiatives, including a community foundation that arranges events and donations throughout the community. Our wellness program hosts walks during lunchtime and fitness challenges and brings in speakers to present to the firm. We've had presentations from a leadership coach, an occupational therapist, an aromatherapist, a yoga instructor, and even the head fitness trainer for the Golden State Warriors cheerleading squad. People think we're crazy to encourage all this stuff, but it pays off tenfold. Our turnover of good people is now incredibly low. Staff morale and productivity is high. This is due, in part, to the breaks these initiatives provide from what is often difficult, tedious work.

It all started, though, with lunch. We had five people back then, so I gave my assistant forty bucks and asked her to go buy sandwiches. We sat in the conference room and ate together. It was simple, and it gave us a chance to bond. It's since grown into a monthly luncheon in which we celebrate birthdays, congratulate the team on big wins, and discuss new ideas for the firm. Almost everyone shows up, and it's a great opportunity to rub elbows and build community within our walls.

You may worry about the cost of social activities. Trust me, I worried about it. We were a growing company that needed our cash for salaries and overhead. We had a million other places we could spend money, but we decided to invest it in culture. That investment wasn't a big deal when it was forty dollars for sandwiches. As the firm grew, we found we were spending $700 on each luncheon. It was getting expensive, so we came up with ideas to make it work without breaking the bank.

We worked with a vendor who has a similar culture to ours. They shared our values, and we loved working together. One day, they happened to be in our office when we were holding the luncheon, so we invited them in. They loved it so much that they asked to sponsor the luncheon every month. Now, they pay the seven hundred-or-so dollars, we remind our team of the value of these vendors, and everyone feels a greater sense of belonging.

INTIMATE BELONGING

A great culture embraces the power of team and group dynamic. As our firm has grown, we've created micro-groups within the larger company, so staff can still access the intimacy of a small group. There are only three to five members in each micro-group. They choose their own name and create their own culture. Most have named themselves for local San Francisco sports teams. We have the Warriors, the Giants, the Raiders, and the Earth-quakes. In one group, a few of the team members are gay; they call themselves Team Queen.

In such small groups, a sense of belonging quickly develops. Members have each other's backs and feel the impact of their colleagues' efforts—or lack thereof. This motivates people to work their hardest every day. It gives them purpose beyond a paycheck. Because we deliberately hire friendly and compassionate people, these groups have not turned into cliques. We've weeded out complainers through our hiring process, as we'll discuss later in this book, and we don't have the "normal" politics that many offices our size endure. Instead, we have friendly people who enjoy a sense of belonging.

PERSONAL GROWTH

At the top of Maslow's hierarchy of needs pyramid sits self-actualization, which comes from achieving one's full potential. In our law firm, we see employees become attuned to the company's mission. They see their work as worthwhile because it contributes to that mission. They feel fulfilled because they know they play a pivotal role in something of importance. It's not easy to reach self-actualization. It requires that the lower tiers of the pyramid be satisfied first. Then, the company must help employees meet their professional and personal goals. Providing constant training and opportunities for improvement is essential.

Karla is a great example of an employee who worked her way up the pyramid, growing our firm in the process. She was nineteen when she started as a legal assistant at another firm. She came to us about ten years into her career, taking a position as the receptionist in our tiny office. She began to handle intakes—talking to prospective clients and trying to bring them on board—and was exceptionally good at it, thanks to her care, compassion, and hunger to learn. She dealt with some impostor syndrome, which is the feeling that you are not good enough for your position. She spent so many years in law firms that looked at her as "just an assistant" that it was often hard for her to see more in her abilities.

I constantly pushed Karla to learn more about the sales process, human psychology, and the human condition. A year or so into her tenure, I gave her Sheryl Sandberg's book *Lean In: Women, Work, and the Will to Lead*. Sandberg is the chief operating officer of Facebook and *Time* magazine once named her one of the most influential people in the world. I wanted Karla to read something by this extremely successful woman in business to see that anything really is possible. I wanted her to develop a mindset more open to possibility. We sent her and several other employees to a personal development seminar. We hired an executive coach to meet with Karla whenever she felt she couldn't come to us with challenges.

Encouraging Karla's personal growth increased her professional development—and vice versa. Karla learned more about herself and grew her self-esteem. At the same time, we encouraged her to actively participate in her job. She refined and documented the processes involved, then taught them to others. We thought this was important as Karla is warm, caring, and driven—in short, a natural leader. She just didn't know she had leadership qualities, so we had to bring them out.

Through all this, Karla's confidence grew, as did her conversion rates, which were far above industry standards. She became manager of the intake team and then the director, spending more time analyzing data on leads and further refining our process. Her department's intake conversion rates are so high that when I hired an outside company to do sales training, they said they'd never heard of a conversion rate as high as ours. I attribute this to Karla's intense dedication and willingness to learn. Her team is incredibly dedicated to her. This is no surprise, as it's clear she cares about them in a significant way. Karla is also now part of our management committee, and she helps guide the firm in major decisions.

When Karla and I had lunch to celebrate her five-year anniversary with our firm, we talked about her journey from receptionist to director and management committee member. She said that if she'd continued working in other jobs, she would probably still be an assistant. Her career growth would not have been possible because she wouldn't have had the opportunity to contribute to her job in the same way, and therefore others wouldn't have seen her abilities. No one would have pushed her personal and professional development, and she would not have seen her own potential.

In our firm, we have several processes in place to ensure employees like Karla can grow to their full potential. One of these is the Failure Log, a simple sheet of paper clipped to every desk. Any time an employee sees an issue or a mistake, they are to write down the issue and a suggested improvement, which then gets discussed with the team. Large process changes follow a different format, but small improvements happen fast and frequently through the Failure Log, which also helps people recognize that mistakes are not fatal and should not be hidden. Our biannual developmental reviews are far more significant, and we have several other growth-oriented ideas, which I'll detail in chapter seven when we discuss processes. All of them, including the Failure Log, serve to empower every employee, from the mailroom guy to the reception-ist to the attorneys.

You simply can't grow your business without growing individuals toward self-actualization. Without growth, employees will leave simply for a change of scenery. They'll stay, though, if they have something to look forward to every day.

AVOIDING HELL ON EARTH

Back when I used to fly around the country meeting big clients, my mother would say, "I'm so proud of you. You're doing so well." I'd respond, "Yes, I've created a perfect hell for myself." In meeting and then exceeding basic human needs, you can prevent your workplace from becoming hell on earth. You won't fall into the trap of luring in new attorneys with empty promises, then revealing the fiery furnace of an unsafe and undisciplined workplace void of friendship or fulfillment. You will honor your commitments, develop trust and society, and grow your firm. You'll create un-poachable employees; those who are esteemed and fulfilled at work cannot be stolen by rival firms. When 71 percent of Americans are looking for a new job at any given time, as discovered in a survey by the nonprofit group Mental Health America and The Faas Foundation, that's a big fucking deal.

Now that you're clear a great culture is about fulfilling and then going beyond basic human needs, you can assess how your company stacks up against the pyramid. Are you creating a perfect hell or something heavenly? To determine that, you must first look to yourself. That's what we'll discuss next.

CHAPTER THREE

NOTHING CHANGES UNLESS YOU CHANGE

"The pretense of knowledge is our most dangerous
vice, because it prevents us from getting any better."
—RYAN HOLIDAY

If you'd told me twenty years ago that I'd be the guy waking up, meditating, and breathing through yoga stretches in my living room, I'd have laughed at you. I wanted to be Gordon Gekko, the stylish corporate raider from the 1987 movie *Wall Street*. Gekko didn't give a shit about anybody. He was "all about bucks, kid." Now, here I am, meditating like a hippie and trying to convince you to be nice. Oh, how I have changed. The world, of course, has also changed in the last twenty years. We're now in an era of instant connectedness and constant distractions. Clients can communicate with us twenty-four hours a day, seven days a week, 365 days a year—and they expect an immediate response. In a busy world, meditation has helped me slow down.

It's less hippy-ish than you might think. I don't have the mental capacity to sit alone in silence, so I use an app called Calm. It takes me through a guided meditation for ten minutes every morning, and it leaves me feeling... calm. In our society, meditation has become a huge phenomenon. Calm is now valued at $1 billion, and there are many other popular meditation apps on the market, including Headspace and Ten Percent Happier. Clearly, I'm not the only person who needs help clearing my head.

I started meditating after reading Tim Ferriss's incredible book *Tribe of Mentors*. It contains interviews with thought leaders and people at the top of their game in a variety of different arenas, including sports, business, tech, literature, and many more. Ferriss posed the same questions to each person and compiled the responses in his book. He asked, "What's one ritual you do every day? Name three books you give to people. If you had a billboard in Times Square, what would it say? What's your personal motto?" He also analyzed the responses to discover commonalities. Almost everyone interviewed said they practice meditation every day. I thought, *Well, fuck. If all these successful people swear by it, I'd better learn how to meditate.*

After trying the app, I discovered meditation isn't some big, mystical thing. It's just about being still and present in the moment and clearing your mind. When your mind is clear, you can acknowledge your body. You can breathe deeply, which has a rejuvenating, creative effect. Meditation is the best way I have found in this busy world to stop and smell the roses. It helps you develop more self-awareness, which is essential for a leader.

PRIMARY REALITY

I used to spend at least ten hours on the phone every day. This wasn't confined to the workweek. Like many lawyers, my work never stopped. I was at it on weekends and holidays. No day was immune. I had the phone practically glued to my face; my brother used to say I should have it surgically attached. For years, I would walk into the office on the phone and head straight to my desk. I'd take calls throughout lunch. I would break important meetings to take calls. It was never-ending.

I didn't realize how much my cell phone prevented in-person connections. I would kind of wave at people as I walked into the office, without appreciating that the device constantly concealed my expression. Some bad news would surface, and an employee would say, "Well, I didn't want to tell you because I didn't know what mood you were in." When people don't know your mood, they assume it must be bad, and bad because of them. That's a scary place to be. Eventually, I realized I had to put the damn phone down. When I arrived at the office, I finished calls in my car and put the phone away before walking in. I said hello to everyone I passed. I still do this today.

When you're the company owner, your mood—or perceived mood—affects every person in your office every minute of their day. Like it or not, people fixate on you. Jim Collins speaks to this in his best-selling book *Good to Great: Why Some Companies Make the Leap...and Others Don't.* He says, "The moment a leader allows himself to become the primary reality people worry about, rather than reality being the primary reality, you have a recipe for mediocrity, or worse." Collins means that if employees spend more time trying to mitigate their boss's mood than managing their workload, the company will never thrive.

It's up to you to shift your employees' focus, but to do so you must first change yourself. Business and peak performance coach Tony Robbins says that the success of a business is 100 percent based on the psychology and the skills of an owner. If you're going to be a great leader, you'd better level-up your skillset. You must be the first to say, "I am ready to change."

Getting off my cell phone and meditating were not the

only things I changed. I was constantly trying to improve my practical skills as an executive. Peter F. Drucker, who passed away in 2005 at ninety-five years old, remains the preeminent thought leader in business management. Although it's unclear where the quote originated, he is credited with the famous saying, "Culture eats strategy for breakfast." Drucker wrote close to forty books on management, fourteen of them after the age of eighty. To me, none of his books are more important than *The Effective Executive: The Definitive Guide to Getting the Right Things Done,* written in 1967. On his podcast, Tim Ferriss once interviewed Jim Collins, considered Drucker's intellectual heir, and commented that he's read *The Effective Executive* at least ten times. Getting great at your job, setting priorities, holding great meetings, and developing talent below you are just some of the essential functions of a great executive covered in the book. If you want to get great at running a firm, get great at your basic core management and leadership duties. This was the mantra that motivated me to progress down this path of change.

EGO HALTS ALL PROGRESS

Change is particularly tricky when it's your name above the door. Partners often name law firms after themselves and plaster those names on the building, the letterhead, business cards, office signs, and everywhere else you can imagine. This can send someone's ego into the stratosphere and inflame the already-oversized personalities that practice law. Trial lawyers are performers. Attorneys are eager to be pillars of the community—and stand in the spotlight that affords. There are so many egos in our industry.

After graduating from law school, I worked for a solo attorney in Phoenix, Arizona. This guy, who we'll call Matthew, had previously been a big-firm go-to lawyer in real estate development. He shifted and became a real estate developer before going broke and starting over as a solo practitioner. Matthew was probably the most difficult boss I ever had. Yelling was a constant thing at his firm, which was a small place with just three of us there. I was constantly scared. My desk faced a wall, and I sat with my back to him. I could barely get out of my chair without him remarking on my work ethic. I was also constantly worried about who he was going to piss off that day outside the office.

He took me to lunch quite often, and on one particular day, we ate at his private club. When we finished, we stood outside waiting for the valet to bring his car around. A woman pulled up and saw the valet wasn't there. She looked at us and said, "I'm running late for a lunch appointment. Would you mind—" She was obviously about to ask if we could let the valet know her keys were on the stand. Before she could finish her sentence, though, Matthew barked, "I'm not your fucking assistant. Wait like everyone else."

I was mortified. I stood there speechless, but not surprised. This superior attitude was a regular thing with him. He was constantly telling me about his amazing work, how he'd built the biggest real estate projects and was the best litigator. He never blamed himself for his bankruptcy and loss of clients. Everything was always someone else's fault. I spent the majority of my time working for him afraid of his next blowup, whether it would be directed at me or not. Even worse than the blowups was the simple fact that he refused to listen. Working on a brief for one of the firm's clients, I chose a well-researched argument that he refused to believe was good law. It took forever to convince him that his position on the topic was no longer viable. He just couldn't accept that he might be wrong. This is ego. The day after I got notice that I'd passed the California bar, I quit.

When you think you're the most important or smartest person in the room, you're inevitably dismissive and often mean to everyone else. This prevents you from hearing others. It disables learning. So many lawyers are caught up in their importance. They may be experts in their area of law and run cases well, but can they deal with people? Do they know how to treat other human beings? If you believe you're all-powerful and all-knowing, you will never be open enough to consider new ways to level-up your skills. That is why the ego is the enemy—the title of Ryan Holiday's book on the subject.

My sincere advice is this: be clear in your own self-assessment. Ask yourself if you truly listen to people. Do you acknowledge there is something to be learned from every interaction? Are you the last to speak in a meeting? Do you respect others' time? If not, ego is likely getting in the way of everything you do. It's halting your progress. *You must drop your ego.* You have to remove it from every equation, or it will destroy your organization. People just don't want to work with a power-crazy asshole.

THE OPPOSITE OF EGO IS VULNERABILITY

Committing to change and expressing gratitude are vital in opposing ego. We discussed gratitude in chapter three as a coping mechanism when you discover brutal truths about your current culture. Gratitude doesn't just help you appreciate the good in your circumstances; it acts in opposition to ego. As a movie buff, I used to love all things Hollywood, and I would find it fascinating to watch gratitude and ego at play at the annual Oscars awards ceremonies. When actors win awards, their acceptance speeches generally fall into two categories. They either get on stage, take their trophy, and say some version of, "Wow, I really am the greatest, aren't I?" or they say, "This award belongs to everyone who helped me get here." The former has ego. The latter shows gratitude.

To remove ego more fully, though, you must go beyond gratitude to a more difficult trait: vulnerability. Vulnerability is admitting you don't know everything. It's owning up to mistakes and accepting you are fallible. It's removing the costume of the big, bad lawyer and being open with others. This is difficult for me. As a child, my grandmother praised my strength and ability to do anything. She called me by a Yiddish phrase which means, "My little lawyer." If she had to return something to a store, she'd send me to get the job done. If she wanted a reservation at a fully booked restaurant, she'd get me to negotiate it. I was proud of her faith in me and never admitted when I failed for fear of disappointing her.

As a breed, lawyers struggle with vulnerability. We're tough. We often think we're infallible. Our thick skin projects an image of strength that, at first glance, seems at odds with vulnerability. People call us sharks and pit bulls and assholes. We're not considered soft and fuzzy. This traditional image of lawyers is starting to change, albeit very slowly. We occasionally now see vulnerability in law firm marketing. John Morgan is an amazing lawyer who openly talks about his family's suffering. His brother became paralyzed at work, and his family had a terrible experience following the accident. He tells this emotional story of wanting to become a lawyer so he could prevent other families from struggling in the same way. And you know what? Emotion drives people more than anything else. His vulnerability sells. Morgan has one of the most successful practices in America.

THE UMBRELLA OF VULNERABILITY

I learned a lot about vulnerability in the workplace from Brené Brown. Her research and writing set the stage for this subject. She teaches that you can't be an effective leader without acting with vulnerability and courage. And let's be clear here: vulnerability does not mean weakness. It's simply opening up to your people, sharing your desires and dreams, expressing your feelings, and showing your weakness. This allows others to connect with you. Any great friendship, partnership, or marriage needs more than just surface talk. It requires the true connection that comes from vulnerability. And if you're busy projecting your power, there won't be space for that necessary vulnerability.

Vulnerability also does not mean revealing everything about your personal life or business decisions. There are boundaries. You get to choose what you'll bring inside the realm of vulnerability, and what you'll keep at bay. That said, I encourage you to consider being generous in what you'll include under the umbrella of vulnerability.

When I got married, I invited some people from our team, and I realized they didn't know much about me outside of work. It was so good for them to see me interact with friends and family. They met my brother, sister, mother, and cousins. They discovered more of my personality and saw me as a person with a life outside the business. This has made it easier for them to connect with, like, and trust me. You can't expect people to trust you unless they've seen your human side.

In the office, vulnerability means being honest about performance and accountability. You might be losing a case and need the team to fully engage so that you can get back on track. The team can't know unless you're honest about the current and past struggles, admitting your failure and accepting the consequences. Sometimes vulnerability means admitting you don't have all the answers. People sometimes come to me for help on subjects I know little about. I say, "Look, I can't tell you I have all the answers, but we do have a process for problem-solving we can use to find the answers." Then, we work through the process of discovering the best answer. I set my ego aside, try a new approach, and work from there.

SELF-CARE FOR SURVIVAL

The day before I started law school, my brother called me to discuss a new approach to improving myself. Neil is seven years my senior and far more accomplished than I could ever aspire to be. He's an M.D., a Ph.D., and is in the Martial Arts Hall of Fame as a multi-degree black belt in Taekwondo and Krav Maga. He's also a little nuts. He has run marathons, done iron mans, and climbed mountains in his bare feet. He used to live in Milwaukee, and every winter, he'd drive down to Lake Michigan, cut a hole in the ice, and jump into the semi-frozen water—for fun. When he called that day, though, it was with some very sane, sage advice.

"The most successful people in my medical school class," he told me, "were those who did something physical every day—even the days we didn't sleep," he said. "Find some routine that clears your head, or you'll never be able to fill it with new stuff. To stay healthy, you'll need both mental and physical energy."

Growing up, I didn't exercise much. I'd watch my brother run miles, and I always thought it looked exhausting. I value his wisdom though, so on the first day of law school, I got up at 6 a.m., put on some running shoes, walked out of my apartment at the corner of Sacramento and Hyde in San Francisco, and ran straight up to the crest of Nob Hill, around the Pacific Union Club, and back to my apartment. The whole run took fifteen minutes. Having never run before, this was about the most I could handle, but I soon worked my way up to a couple of miles a day. I never enjoyed running, but I did love the beautiful early morning views as I ran along San Francisco's waterfront. It was a glorious way to start each day, and the time for reflection was essential in those difficult law school days. I eventually ditched running, but I still do something physical each morning, whether it's twenty minutes of yoga or a two-hour session at the gym.

Starting and running a business is intense and difficult. It takes an enormous amount of energy. It's a marathon, not a sprint. You can only survive the intensity and effort required if you're taking care of yourself. Taking down your ego and being vulnerable with yourself lets you see where you are weakest. Then, you can spend time on self-care to shore up those weaknesses.

Self-care can be exercise, like running or going to the gym. It can be something more meditative, such as practicing yoga or hiking. It could be golf, reading, sailing, painting, or any kind of hobby. Do whatever speaks to you, and try to make it physical. Try to make it something that requires total concentration, something that focuses your mind completely away from the stresses of the business. If you try something and don't love it, pivot to another activity. The point is this: you must find a hobby. Hobbies clear the mind; a clear mind is a breeding ground for creativity, and creativity creates business growth. Hobbies also generate energy. They are essential to replenish the mind, body, and soul. They provide nourishment for the long, intense hours of focus required to build a successful business.

I meditate every morning, try to get to the gym each day, and play a lot of golf. I do this by carefully choosing my schedule. I limit my meetings. I'm very disciplined in planning my days with enough space to care for myself. If I don't care for myself, I can't care for anyone else. And we know that the leader's job is to care for their employees, so the employees can care for the clients, and the clients can care for everyone.

I also spend a considerable amount of time in Costa Rica and was inspired to do so by John Morgan, who founded Morgan & Morgan, one of the largest personal injury firms in the country. They sign thousands of cases a month. Morgan is a pioneer who proves that small firms can transform when they apply basic business principles to their practice. In Morgan's book *You Can't Teach Hungry: Creating the Multimillion Dollar Law Firm*, he talks about taking a couple of weeks every January to get away from it all, clear his head, and work on ideas for his firm. If you haven't read this book, get it. Seriously. It's essential to any lawyer trying to grow a firm. Morgan's words inspired me to acknowledge when I needed a break to recharge. When I started taking trips to Costa Rica, I found the mental space to reflect, be creative, practice gratitude, and truly be calm.

CALM IS A SUPERPOWER

A lot of leaders have been hotheads, but in today's workplace, calm leadership is a necessity. Calm is also a superpower. I don't recall where I first heard this sentiment, but I love how it succinctly conveys the choice to engage the power of a calm response in any given situation.

Viktor Frankl was a Nazi concentration camp prisoner who understands the power of choosing your reactions. He wrote about this concept in his book *Man's Search for Meaning*, which has sold more than 12 million copies worldwide and was named one of the ten most influential books in the United States by the Library of Congress. Frankl is credited with saying, "Between stimulus and response there is a space. In that space is our power to choose our response. In our response lies our growth and our freedom." This is, in essence, the prayer of Alcoholics Anonymous, originally written by Reinhold Niebuhr. It says, "God grant me the serenity to accept the things I cannot change, courage to change the things I can, and the wisdom to know the difference." Both quotes speak of identifying what you cannot change and choosing your reaction to them. I suggest business owners choose to be calm.

Often, leaders are too high-energy. Calm isn't in their nature; it certainly is not in mine. This is a common challenge. I would get so agitated by simple things such as timekeeping. At work, I watched the clock. If an employee was due at 8:30 a.m. and arrived at 8:31 a.m., I'd haul them into my office.

"Why the fuck are you getting in at 8:31?" I'd ask. "This is law. We have to be on time. We need to meet deadlines. A judge will be harsher with you than I am."

I know from experience that judges are strict time-keepers. Just days after 9/11, I had an 8 a.m. case at the Northern District Court in San Francisco. Following the attacks, courts nationwide had closed, and this was their first-day reopening. I arrived early to find a huge line of people waiting to enter the building. It took forever to get through the metal detectors, up the elevator, and into the courtroom. I walked in as the second hand on the court-room clock swept past the top of the minute, announcing it was officially after 8 a.m. "Mr. Farber, you're late," said the judge. "Sit down. You will not be allowed to argue on behalf of your client today." I lost the case and had to appeal the ruling.

CHOOSE WHAT MATTERS

In our office, I acted just like that judge. I felt justified because this was law. The system operated on timeliness. It was my partner, Bilal, who helped change my attitude and approach. He'd say, "Look, Eric, these people are working hard for us. You can't be so harsh. Don't get so upset every time things go wrong. And if someone is a little late, that doesn't count as 'going wrong,' anyway." He convinced me to choose what matters.

Eventually, I realized pissing off my staff for the sake of one minute did not matter. They were good people who did their jobs well. They cared for our clients. They were dedicated, motivated, and trustworthy, so what did it matter if they were a few minutes late because they had car troubles? If you've hired the right people, the reason for their lateness may not even be your business. Good people deserve to be trusted, not micromanaged and berated.

Constant lateness is a different creature. That *is* your business. We recently had an employee show up late thirty-one times over a two-month period. We asked what was going on, and if we could make an adjustment to accommodate her kids' school drop-off. Many of our assistants have a flex start time, which allows them to choose when they come in because we understand everyone's lives are different. This chronically late employee gave no explanations and continued to be late after significant warnings. Unfortunately, we had to fire her.

Bilal helped me see that, chronic conditions aside, I had

to chill the fuck out. I needed to react calmly when I saw employees arriving late or behaving in ways I wouldn't. I considered an Epictetus quote, which offers my favorite version of this sentiment. He said, "In life our first job is this, to divide and distinguish things into two categories: externals I cannot control, but the choices I make with regard to them I do control. Where will I find good and bad? In me, in my choices."

Become a manager of change. Choose to approach challenges with calm intention. When you are going through growth, not everything will be perfect. In fact, in drastic growth, it will feel like something is going wrong daily or even hourly. Approach these challenges with calm intention. It's okay if you don't know what to do with them. Take time to think through the issues. Talk with and listen to your team. If you have the right people with you, as we'll discuss in later chapters, they will help you through the difficult times.

MEDITATE TO INVOKE CALM *AND* CREATIVITY

I choose to meditate every morning. It's become one of my most calming self-care rituals. It helps me be more creative in my business ideas, which is essential in being able to pivot. Business pivots are required when the working environment changes. The personal injury industry has a huge change on the horizon in the form of self-driving cars. These computer-driven vehicles will decimate the car accident business because 80 percent of vehicle collisions are due to human error. Take the humans out of driving, and you have no more accidents. In the past few years, at least a dozen companies have emerged trying to supplant small family law matters with online systems. Ross Intelligence, the leader in lawyer artificial intelligence, is already being used by more than fifty large law firms to do legal research and write briefs. The process of forming corporations and LLCs for small businesses was irreversibly changed with the launch of LegalZoom, the massive, online, do-it-yourself legal system. These changes and pivots in business are all around us. You just have to look to see them. Outside of law, Apple began making personal computers in 1976. It is now a phone business, a music distribution service, an e-book and movie retailer, and has even entered the credit card business.

You must constantly be creative, so you can pivot to accommodate environmental changes. The business you're in today may not be your business of tomorrow. You must maintain a clear enough mind to innovate— or you simply won't keep up. I worked hard to make good choices, become less reactive, and encourage my own creativity. This kept me calm, which created more mental space to analyze issues. It stopped me from feeling overwhelmed.

CHANGE FOR SUCCESS

It is hard to argue with reality. There are going to be facts that you encounter in your law firm that may be particularly brutal, but they are facts. There are people that you will need to get rid of, processes that may be terrible and need changing, and those changes may take months. These things might require hard work and a lot of it, but one thing is for certain. Ignoring these facts won't make them go away. You must confront them.

As the Stoic philosopher Marcus Aurelius famously said, "The obstacle in the way is the way." Ego will derail you; attending to the challenge of ego is the path to success. You must set aside your ego and embrace vulnerability. Attend to your mental and physical health and use calm as a superpower for clarity and creativity. This is how you change into a true leader. That sure as hell was true for me. Peter F. Drucker said, "Leadership is the lifting of a man's vision to higher sites, the raising of a man's performance to a higher standard, the building of a man's personality beyond its normal limitations." We have taken our firm beyond its normal limitations. Most attorneys don't make a great living. According to the US Bureau of Labor Statistics, the average lawyer in America earns $120,000 per year. That's the average. We booked seven figures in less than eighteen months. Like us, you can take your firm beyond its normal limitations if you are willing to change. Personal change is an ongoing process, but once you are aware of your own necessary growth, you can start to look out to your firm.

CHAPTER FOUR

DEFINE YOUR CURRENT CULTURE

"We have two ears and one mouth, so that we can listen twice as much as we speak."

—EPICTETUS

I was a terrible listener for most of my life. As a child, I had wonderfully supportive parents and teachers who always told me how smart I was. They put me in the advanced classes. They built my confidence. As I grew, so did my ego. I thought I knew everything, so I didn't need to listen to anybody. This is why I was such a lousy law student. I thought I knew more than enough to get going in the world, and I didn't want to wait. I was impatient. I saw nothing to be gained from sitting in dreary rooms listening to lectures.

When I began building this business, I realized I couldn't

know everything about running a firm. It was impossible. That's when I started to understand that it is more important to listen than to talk. I started listening to business experts. I read every business book I could and was absolutely open to the ideas within them. The concepts I learned began to fuse together like quilt patches, each unique but joining seamlessly with the others. They expanded into a large blanket that became our company culture. At the center of the patchwork were the ideas of active listening and trust-building. Everything else—vulnerability, courage, and personal development—spun out from these key concepts.

I worked hard to improve my listening skills. I wanted to hear what employees were saying, so I could understand the state of the business. You must listen to what is happening in your firm so that you can address your unique cultural issues. And yes—your company does have a culture, even if you haven't deliberately cultivated one. Cultures form wherever people gather, with or without considered and intentional guidance.

Without skillful listening, it's difficult to define your current culture. You may have one impression, employees might tell you something else, and the truth may differ from that. It's extraordinarily important to discover that truth, though. When your car breaks down, you must diagnose the issue so you can fix the problem. You don't want to invest time and energy changing a hose when you actually have a flat tire. You cannot address the cultural challenges in your firm without first knowing what they are.

Unfortunately, it's easy to lose touch with your company's culture as the business grows and you rise through the ranks. Attorneys often move from being solo practitioners to managing a small staff, to leading a larger team, and every step up the ladder is a step away from awareness of the firm's culture. Non-attorneys may start as an assistant and move through the ranks into management.

Some time ago, Irving, our director of operations, experienced this. He was our first employee and joined us as an assistant. As we brought in more staff, Irving would tell Bilal and me what other employees were saying around the watercooler. He'd share the office gossip and help us understand what employees thought about the firm. We made a lot of decisions and changes based on those discussions. Over the years, he worked his way up the ranks, and we promoted him to director of operations. That was when he noticed a change. Not too long after his promotion, we looked to Irving for an office gossip update. He shrugged his shoulders and laughed.

"I don't know," he said. "No one tells me anything anymore."

"You see how it feels?" I said. "You're a boss now. No one will just tell you the truth anymore. You have to listen more carefully." Now, this was some time ago. We weren't—and certainly still are not—perfect. As we've grown as leaders, though, we've tried to create a culture in which staff feel safe enough to share their thoughts with the leaders. We didn't have this when Irving was first promoted. That meant continuous listening was more important than ever. It is not enough to listen a few times. As we grow, as the firm fluctuates, as people get promoted and dynamics shift, we must continue to actively listen, so we don't lose touch with the company's culture. Irving has long since settled into his role and is now very good at tuning into the state of the firm. He can sense when the energy of a particular department feels low. He is attuned to his surroundings because he listens.

THE COMMON CULTURE

We can find clues as to the state of your company's culture by considering law firms in general. In the best-selling book *Great Mondays: How to Design a Company Culture Employees Love*, author Josh Levine suggests that service organizations—which include law firms—have cultures defined by their owner, who is usually too busy to consider it. Levine runs a culture design firm in Berkeley, California. I recently met with him for coffee, and I asked him about law practices. He said that in small- to mid-sized firms with fewer than fifty people, there is generally a cohesive culture which reflects the owner. At this size, a firm's owner is highly involved in its everyday function. Employees see their presence and look to them for clues about what will help them succeed there.

Most law firms are led by attorneys who were, throughout their careers, indoctrinated in cultures of hierarchy and insecurity. We've already discussed the hierarchical caste system that occurs between attorneys and support staff. The adversarial attitude in most firms adds to this divisiveness. It's in a lawyer's nature to fight for people, for justice, for victory. The inclination to argue often seeps into the internal culture and makes it easy for relationships to rupture. Generally, in small businesses, the personality of the owner will drive the culture. Like attracts like. If the owner's values are misaligned, it is likely that other people in the organization will be misaligned. If the owner values customer service, it will likely become a customer-service-centered organization. If the owner is a jerk, there will probably be other jerks around.

Many leaders sense their employees are not committed to the firm and overpay to attempt to keep people in their jobs. We do need to pay enough to cover employees' basic needs for shelter, food, and warmth, but overpaying does not compensate for poor culture. A generous paycheck may keep an employee on board, but without the support of a positive culture, they will not give the company 100 percent of themselves. Their physiological human needs—those on the bottom of Maslow's hierarchy—will be met, but the employee will still feel insecure. That will drive them to disengage. Then, they are vulnerable to being poached by other employers. Can you imagine, though, if you overpaid and had a great culture? You'd have un-poachable employees, and your company would grow tenfold every year.

LEARN TO LISTEN

For insights into the current culture of your specific law firm, you must learn to listen. If you're like me and almost everyone else on the planet, you were never taught to listen. When we were young, we learned to read and write. We sat in classrooms repeating writing exercises until we could perfectly pen our names, cross our t's, and dot our i's. From an even earlier age, our parents stood over us, patiently awaiting our first words. We listened to their ridiculous baby noises. We listened, even though we were never taught how. Perhaps because it comes easy and early, listening has never been taught. It's not part of our school curriculums or societal expectations. But listening *well* is not easy.

One of my favorite movies is *Pulp Fiction* by writer and director Quentin Tarantino. I still remember seeing it in theaters shortly after law school. It was certainly a groundbreaking film that took the world by storm. It contained a scene between Uma Thurman and John Travolta that always stuck with me. Travolta's character, Vincent Vega, is tasked with taking the boss's wife, Mia Wallace—played by Thurman—to dinner. Mia Wallace is sitting across from Vincent, and she bluntly asks, "When in conversation, do you listen, or do you just wait to talk?" We can learn a lot from this short and brilliant piece of dialogue because it speaks to a universal truth. At any point in a conversation, most people are not listening. They are part-listening and part-waiting to talk. If you're paying attention with a small portion of your brain, you will inevitably miss some of what is said.

For a more highbrow discussion of listening, we can look to the Dalai Lama. He said, "Listening is a human quality that few people have mastered. When you talk, you are only repeating what you already know." If we don't want to get stuck in the cycle of repeating what we think we know, we must master listening.

In the last five years, I have attempted to do just that. It is not easy. In fact, it's really fucking hard. Like most people, as soon as I hear a problem, I start throwing together a solution in my mind. Listening means stopping those mental acrobatics and, instead, asking questions. I have become considerably better at listening to my team—

whom I hired, after all, to run things. Sure, they execute my vision for customer service, branding, marketing, and so on, but they do the real work, and the only way to learn about my firm is to listen to the people doing the real work every day.

My meditation practice made me a better listener. Merely being quiet for a few minutes every day has made me more attuned to activity around me. I practiced speaking last in meetings. I listened, paused, and asked questions before jumping into solutions. I posed issues to my team and guided them to ask each other questions, so we could all listen and narrow down potential solutions and consequences together. I taught them to listen, as I learned to do the same.

This process of asking questions and guiding to solutions can lead to a lot of rabbit holes. When you're in a time of scarcity, lengthening the decision-making process seems crazy, I know. If you truly don't have enough time, resources, or people, pick and choose your listening battles. Identify the most important issues, use this technique with them, and stick with the fast, dictator process elsewhere. Don't write off listening in every area because you don't have time in all areas. You've got to make the time. That might require dropping a few cases, slowing down, and creating time to breathe. A good leader carves out that time. Just break the habit somewhere and increase your efforts incrementally. You'll notice this creates good solutions that everyone buys into. For your team, this creates a sense of self-esteem and accomplishment—which is precisely what you're trying to achieve.

We paid particular attention to communication via text messages and email. Those can be particularly tricky because, in written form, a person's true intention doesn't always come through. Any time we suspected miscommunication was occurring, we picked up the phone to speak—and listen—in real time. My general rule is that three back-and-forth emails signify a phone call is necessary to get on the same page. Talking gives the conversation space. It lets you easily repeat a statement back to the speaker to ensure you understood. You can pause after they've spoken to process your thoughts, and you can ask questions to clarify. In-person conversations allow you to listen and understand in real time, and be heard and understood just as fast.

We also teach and discuss active listening with our team. When this becomes a company habit, something else happens. You build trust. When people feel heard, they believe you care. When they think you care, they want to work for you. They're eager to do business together. They start to bring the best version of themselves to work every day, and isn't that what you really want?

I have worked on active listening more than any other skill. It's helped me become a trusted leader, a more effective marketer, and a better Sherpa of my firm's client experience. When I really listened, I could hear what my employees said was important. I could better understand the marketplace we operate within, and the needs of our clients.

There are experts all around you, waiting to be heard. You just have to listen. It is the single most effective tool in creating a better culture. Not only does it allow you to hear other people, but it also lets others feel heard, which develops trust. Listening makes conversations easier, calmer, and more productive.

THEN, TALK

When you're confident you are capable of really listening, you can start to ask questions about your company's culture. You should ask a lot of questions. Talk to people in any way, shape, or form. Bring them into the fold. Do it formally and informally. Be curious at every opportunity.

We have monthly company surveys, and I'm very proud of them. Our payroll company manages the process. They ask different questions each month, all intended to gauge how well we satisfy our employees' human needs. They cover areas including pay rates, accommodation, workspace, workload, management and micromanagement, happiness, fulfillment, and prospects. As I write, our most recent survey showed 100 percent of employees were happy or very happy at work.

Our first questionnaire was less sophisticated than our current process but covered many of the same interest areas. Bilal conducted it without consulting me. He probably knew I wouldn't be on board. The idea terrified me. I didn't want to know how bad a boss I was, and how poorly I was running the company. I didn't want to confront the brutal facts. Thanks to Bilal's efforts, though, I did discover that our employees were not very happy. The survey results weren't good. At least, that's what I thought. Bilal has a more positive nature, and he didn't think our responses were so disastrous. Back then, though, I struggled to see the glass as half full. I just thought, "Fuck. What's wrong with me?"

We didn't let that deter us, though. We began to ask tough questions and face sometimes brutal responses on a regular basis. Curiosity is one of the greatest human traits, and we got really curious about our employees' opinions. We approached it as a problem to be solved. Einstein said, "If I had an hour to solve a problem, I'd spend fifty-five minutes thinking about the problem, and five minutes thinking about the solutions." That means he spent the vast majority of time asking questions about problems.

That is the only way of reaching solutions. You must ask questions, lots of questions, and ensure they are the right ones. The wrong questions don't lead to real solutions.

The question of *the right questions* is very particular to lawyers. In law school, we're taught to use cross-examination as a tool. We ask questions deliberately crafted to lead down a particular path. These "leading questions" do not help when we're trying to elicit answers that provide honest insights into our company culture. Instead, we must be willing to ask open questions, truly listen to the answers, and dig deep to get to the right solution. Our payroll company, who manages our questionnaires, asks a wide range of questions, all deliberately engineered to evoke honest responses. Now, I calmly look forward to our survey results, as I know they'll provide insights into what's not working and where we can improve.

The method of question-asking doesn't matter, but to get an accurate measure of the company's current culture, you have to ask questions that elicit honest answers. Create your own questions, but make sure they are probing and curiosity-driven, to encourage open answers. *How do you feel at work? Are you happy here? Do you spend time with colleagues outside of the office? What kind of future do you see yourself having here?* Ask about every aspect of a person's work so you can get a good pulse on their experience. You're looking for a sense of your employees' satisfaction—or lack thereof.

Many of your questions will inevitably relate to the individual more so than the company. This may seem strange when you're looking for clues about the company's culture. But a company is comprised of individuals. They are one and the same. When a person feels accomplished, the company accomplishes its goals. This is why you must look to the people in your firm to define your culture.

The first time you ask these questions, you'll quickly get a sense of your company's culture. Then, you'll ask again a month later, and track the metrics that emerge. As you gather this information, you may quickly see a common theme, or you might need much longer to discover what's happening. Tuning into your company's culture is a muscle that develops with use. Now, I can walk into our office and sense even a slight shift in the cultural dynamic. When things are off, there's no excitement in the air. There's no push. If I hear a lawyer's phone ringing off the hook during lunch, I know something is wrong. I can spot it in the balance sheet, too. When people are struggling, performance and profitability drop. That's why I know it's time for a group happy hour to get everyone talking again. If my sixth sense tells me one person is struggling, I'll ask, "What's wrong?" They'll say, "How the hell did you know something is up?" And they'll go on to share their struggle.

Maybe they're running too many cases or haven't taken a vacation in forever. Perhaps they can't return all their phone calls or service clients as they'd like. When you're attuned to your company's culture, you can sense these issues almost immediately and address them. Then, you take care of your employees, they care for the clients, and the clients take care of everyone.

GRATITUDE

As you define your company's current culture, you might have to face some brutal truths. Whatever you uncover, be grateful. These discoveries will help you grow. In *The Hero's Journey*, Joseph Campbell says the dark cave you do not wish to enter holds the treasure you seek. If you're hearing shitty stuff from your employees, you might feel like you're in a dark place. Gratitude is vital to growth, though. It helps you see what's working and build on it. It lets you face the day knowing all is not bad. It provides a launchpad for turning negatives into positives. It's not easy and it's a constant work in progress for me personally and for our firm, but it is worth the effort.

We've been experimenting with processes to help employees practice gratitude. When someone joins our firm, we ask them to complete a process we call The 30-Day Email. This is a simple practice that requires they email their team lead at the end of every day for their first thirty days. The email follows a clear format. First, they detail what they accomplished that day. Then, they outline any challenges that arose or questions they may have. Lastly, they dedicate their next day to someone to whom they're grateful. They might say, "I dedicate my work tomorrow to my father who encouraged me to become a lawyer," or, "I dedicate this day to my high school English teacher who never gave up on me."

By beginning their employment with this, we jump-start the learning process. It lets a new employee recognize their accomplishments each day and ask questions in a safe environment. It teaches them that questions, challenges, and failures are absolutely okay. It also helps their department leader coach them, as we'll discuss more in chapter nine. The gratitude element of the email is an addition we've played with to help people see their own north star each day. Dedicating their day to their kids or grandparents or a sick friend, for example, can be a powerful motivator.

This recall to purpose is particularly important in law firms, as we deal with clients in difficult times. In workers' compensation, our people are injured. They're going through lawsuits. They're fucking stressed. We're not talking sunshine, roses, and rainbows on calls with clients. Sometimes, they get frustrated and angry. They might be downright nasty. You must help employees look past this and feel grateful they are in that office. And that can be as simple as a quick statement of gratitude at the end of a difficult day.

After thirty days of these emails, many employees have developed a habit of gratitude. We encourage them to continue this throughout their employment. We also ask them to celebrate small wins with us. Of course, we mark the big wins, but the small accomplishments are almost more important. Frequently celebrations provide opportunities to reflect and be grateful for the progress made.

Another way in which we encourage consistent expressions of gratitude is our "bonusing" system. It's an online program where employees can log on and leave a comment thanking their colleague for handling a difficult client on their behalf, or whatever it is they're grateful for. With their comment, they give out bonus points to each other. Each employee has one hundred bonusing points a month that they can distribute as they like. The only caveat is that they must explain how the coworker earned those points and why they are grateful for that coworker's actions. Employees who receive bonusing points can convert them into cash and gift cards. One of the highest earners in this program used bonusing points to buy a couple of roundtrip tickets on Southwest Airlines.

As a company, we pay about $1,000 a month for this service. It's not cheap, but it is an important investment. It encourages team, community, and gratitude far more than we could by cajoling employees ourselves. When an employee leaves a thank-you to another coworker, everyone sees it and gets inspired by their colleague's efforts. These small celebrations literally reward positive behavior and encourage more of the same.

Learning to listen was a profound personal change, which was essential in defining our company's culture. Without *really* listening, I would've remained ignorant of the areas in which we needed to improve. Nothing would've changed. When I defined our culture, I understood what we were working with. This wasn't exactly fun, and it likely won't be a thrill ride for you. However, it is a necessary step. With the information you'll gather and the gratitude you'll practice, you'll be ready to establish your values, improve your culture, and grow your firm.

CHAPTER FIVE

ENVISION YOUR VALUES

*"Culture, by its very definition, isn't the work of
being right. It's the work of being in sync."*
—SETH GODIN

When I started this business, I accidentally joined the 4
a.m. club. Mark Wahlberg, who was at one point reportedly the world's best-paid actor, and Tim Cook, the CEO
of Apple, are part of this club, as are many CEOs, athletes,
and artists. Dwayne "The Rock" Johnson, who topped
Forbes' 2019 list of highest paid actors, is also a member.
He even created an app, appropriately named "The Rock
Clock," to help others achieve this goal. Unfortunately,
being a member of the 4 a.m. club does not mean I'm
meeting these legends under the cloak of darkness.
Rather, we each rise at 4 a.m. to allow for time to work,
think, reflect, and be creative in the stillness before the
world wakes with all its distractions.

I never intended to wake up that early every day. It was pure stress and anxiety that opened my eyes while it was still dark outside. I would try to fall back asleep, but the weight of overwhelm pressed down on my chest and I eventually gave up the fight. By the end of the next day, I was so exhausted that I generally fell back into bed and was asleep by 9 p.m. Even if stress remained at bay, I still woke at 4 a.m. because I'd had a solid seven hours of sleep. I laid in bed, staring at the ceiling, hearing every creak of the house, and thinking, "What the hell am I doing?" Much of the time, I felt lost at work. I had no idea how to be a good boss or create the firm I envisioned.

Eventually, I stopped staring at that stupid ceiling, got out of bed, and used the time to get curious about my business. I read business articles and research papers. I thought about processes and how we could better serve clients. I considered priorities and the value of various tasks. I reflected on our firm's efforts. Then, when the sun rose and the office opened, I arrived at work with newfound insights and ideas.

Every successful leader I know spends an enormous amount of time in thoughtful reflection. It is hard, lonely work in those dark hours. However, for busy people, it is often the only opportunity to sit alone and reflect on the state of the business. It's a calm space in which you can escape the phone calls, briefs to get out, multiple meetings, and court appearances. Do you have to do this at the crack of dawn? Probably. This culture work and business building does not happen on its own; you must find time for it, or you will be in the exact same place in ten years. If the only calm time available is from 4 to 6 a.m. before hitting the gym, so be it. The stillness of the early morning allows creativity to soar. It is the perfect time to consider how to grow your business and turn it into the place you envision. At this point, you're essentially running two businesses: the firm as it currently is, and the firm you are becoming. This takes a great deal of time, so these quiet, early morning hours provide the time required to craft the next steps to merge the current business into the future one. Ryan Holiday talks about the practice of creating routine and ritual in his book *Stillness Is the Key*, and my early morning stillness has truly been a key contributor to our success. This ritual of waking up in the quiet stillness to think, contemplate, read, and learn is one of the biggest factors.

AN EXCITING OPPORTUNITY

A company's mission and values are the north stars that remind everyone of why they come to work each day. When our employees use the online bonusing system I discussed in the previous chapter, they can assign colleagues bonus points. When doing so, they are required to comment on how the colleague's actions relate to our company's values. They use a hashtag to reference the relevant value—for example, "Jane stayed late to help me file paperwork for Mr. Smith's case, even though Mr. Smith isn't her client. #betterteam." Our employees know our values because we plaster them everywhere. They are displayed in the office, on our website, in our job postings and onboarding documents, and many other places.

Here are our values:

- Deliver world-class customer service.
- Act with empathy.
- Be driven to get more done.
- Live in a growth mindset.
- Be vulnerable.
- Foster team and community.
- Be honest and transparent.
- Set and follow high standards.
- Work is important and provides meaning in our lives.
- A better me = a better you = a better us.

If you don't have a mission statement and stated core values, you're not alone. I've heard that only 10 percent of organizations have a documented set of values. It is your responsibility, however, to define your firm's values, and it should be an exciting prospect. You have the opportunity to instill your personal values in the organization and build a culture that lives those values.

If you believe in growth and an open mindset, for example, you can adopt these as company values, and create programs that promote growth and openness. You'll then develop a company culture that is constantly open and growing and making you proud. Being clear on your values encourages everyone around you to live into them. If you announce that your firm values community, you are more likely to find ways of contributing to your community. If you declare well-being is important, you will find ways to improve the well-being of everyone with whom you work.

Openly adopting your personal values into your organization can make big changes happen fast. Applicants for new positions will choose you because they share those values. You'll attract vendors who want to develop those values in the community. You'll get more clients who appreciate those aspects of their service providers. Very soon, you will become an extended group with a shared mission of living those values.

VISION OUT THE FUTURE

Before you can document your mission, values, and future, you must first get clear on what they are. I call this process *visioning out*. A leader is the person who sets the company's vision. You could look ninety days into the future, envisioning the firm after you've fixed a customer service issue, or a year ahead as you test a new marketing or cultural initiative, or even further. The timeline itself matters less than the values you imagine.

As a member of the 4 a.m. club, I have found at least two hours each morning to work on visioning out the present and future of the firm. I thought about what I wanted for our customer experience, finances, processes, systems, procedures, growth, and, most importantly, our employees. In the early days of this practice, I'd get a brilliant idea and shoot off an email to the team at five in the morning. I realized most people keep their phone nearby when they sleep, and I was waking them up. It caused them anxiety. That was not my intention. I felt awful when I realized the effects of my early morning emails. I began to write down my thoughts and arrange meetings to review them. This simple act of holding emails back and discussing ideas in person made us more humanistic. It also gave me more time to reflect on the subject matter. Often, I answered my question before the scheduled meeting or decided the idea wasn't that brilliant and wasn't worth bothering anyone over anyway. The more I reflected in these quiet moments, the easier it became to see creative solutions to our challenges. I was able to plan realistic pathways to success that I previously would have thought unobtainable. It helped me imagine a future for our firm in which we grew faster, profited more, and better served everyone involved.

These early morning hours were not restricted to planning for the future. I also used the time to prepare for disasters. As we became bigger, my anxiety began to shift from immediate issues to "what ifs." What if we lost a key employee? What if our marketing suddenly stopped working? What if something brought the company crashing down? This anxiety led me to create a list of things that could go wrong, and I worked to solve them before they happened. I felt like I was creating our version of that flyer you find in the back of airplane seats—the one that outlines escape routes in case of emergency. For everything that could go wrong in our firm, I created an escape plan. These morning planning sessions gave me time to do this with a clear, calm mind, long before issues occurred. It let me create a personalized business guidebook written by my calmer, smarter self. I found great reassurance knowing this was available if something disastrous happened.

These disastrous events don't have to be anyone's "fault." After seeing Florida hammered by severe hurricanes, we decided to create an emergency plan we could use in the event of a natural disaster. Irving, our director of operations, spent several days developing a solid plan to continue serving clients if our office was shut down or, God forbid, destroyed. Within a week of training our staff in this plan, it happened. Wildfires approached, and we were given two hours' notice that we would lose power for five days as authorities struggled to protect infrastructure. The team rallied to execute our new plan. Ten minutes before we evacuated the building, we were notified that the power cut had been canceled. We could stay. It was a rollercoaster experience that we were able to ride out *because we had a plan in place*. Later, *Inc.* magazine interviewed us about this, recognizing how important it is for businesses to be prepared for emergencies.

I shared my "in case of emergency" list with my direct team, which allowed Irving to use his excellent knowledge and ideas to create an actionable plan. You should share your list with your direct reports, too. It will calm you and them, as they are assured yours is a company that thinks ahead in good times *and* in bad. They will know they have a disciplined leader running a disciplined organization.

Whether my early morning ideas dealt with immediate issues, strategized for the future, or planned for emergencies, I crafted and refined them, then shared them with our team. They all exemplified our core values, and I let the team know that living below those values would not be accepted. I created processes, as we'll discuss in chapter seven, to live into our values. We did start living those values and continue to do so today. It triggered our enormous growth in profit and humanity. The experience taught me that you can't create the future until you have envisioned it. The changes I made in learning to listen, connecting to my own values, and making time for visioning out were essential to this process. It showed me that even more change was necessary.

CHAPTER SIX

THE RIGHT PEOPLE IN THE RIGHT SEATS

"Associate with people who are likely to improve you."
—SENECA THE YOUNGER

There are many versions of the above quote by Seneca the Younger. In 1901, Andrew Carnegie, the early American industrialist and philanthropist (and one of the richest Americans in history), said that he wanted his tombstone to read, "Here lies a man who knew how to enlist in his service better men than himself." More recently, Tim Ferriss, author of *The 4-Hour Workweek: Escape 9-5, Live Anywhere, and Join the New Rich,* said if he could put anything on a billboard, it would be, "You are the average of the five people you most associate with." Business coach Tony Robbins calls this concept "proximity" and even sells a private program for more than $60,000 a year based on it. The team you surround yourself with, the people you trust to carry out the company's mission, will make or break you.

It took many years for us to figure this out. In the early days, we knew we weren't surrounding ourselves with the right people. We brought in too many staff who didn't share our values, because we simply didn't know how to find those who did. We were hiring out of desperation, bringing in anyone who'd accept the low wages we paid. We were lucky to stumble across some excellent people, but we had no deliberate process for consistently finding great employees.

Back then, our hiring process went like this: We'd put out an ad for a vacant position and get a bunch of resumes submitted. We'd scan through them and pick out anyone with some relevant experience in our area of law. Then, we'd invite them in for an interview. Sometimes they'd show up and sometimes they wouldn't. For those who bothered to show up, we'd tell them all the amazing things about our company, ask a question or two about their previous experience, and tell them more about what a great place we were. Then, we'd ask, "Does this sound like somewhere you want to work?" They, of course, would say yes. We'd negotiate the lowest salary we could and have them start as soon as possible.

Everything about this was wrong. In this chapter, I'll

share the many lessons I learned from this outdated hiring process. I'll tell you about the changes we made to consistently get the right people into the right seats. Let's start, though, by discussing why it's so disastrous to hire the wrong people—those who don't share the values you envisioned in chapter four. Many law firm owners have a vague sense that the wrong people are bad for business but haven't taken the time to understand why this is true.

THE POWER OF THE WRONG PERSON

A group of great people working together can grow your business exponentially. However, all it takes to close the doors is one bad person. It is vital that a business builds a strong team, but when you're desperate to hire help, it's easy to let the wrong person slip through the doors. That, I believe, is what happened at a small but successful franchise of Papa John's pizzeria. Here's the story, as I heard it.

Minhee Cho, a Korean-American woman, ordered a small pepperoni pizza at one of Papa John's New York branches. She had a friendly chat with the teenager who took her order and handed over a receipt. Cho looked at the receipt and saw something that shocked her. Under customer name, it said, "lady chinky eyes." Cho tweeted a picture of the racial slur with the comment, "Hey @Papa-Johns, just FYI my name isn't 'lady chinky eyes.'" It went viral. The image was viewed more than 200,000 times.

Papa John's apologized and fired the employee—who the store's owner reportedly described as misguided by "hip hop culture"—but it was not enough. Nationwide, customers began a boycott. Papa John's immediately went to protect the brand, apologizing profusely through Twitter and other social media channels to save the company.

It's said that a person can send a tweet in Taiwan and shutter a company in Chicago. In today's world, the actions of one misguided person spread fast and wide, but responsibility does not sit solely with that person. A *Business Insider* report of the Papa John's incident said, "There's fault lying in Papa John's employee screening process. Every once in a while you hire an idiot, and that one little mistake can hurt a multi-million dollar brand."

Even if you escape the fate of Papa John's, having to fire anyone is detrimental to business. It's likely a lesser evil than keeping a bad person on board, but turnover, both employer-led and employee-led, is a business killer. It's enormously expensive to hire and train new employees. Every time someone walks out the door, you lose months of traction, institutional knowledge, and client satisfaction. Focusing on culture keeps the right people around and the wrong people out. That's essential when consistency in your team is a critical factor in growth.

That consistency is difficult to create when 71 percent

of employees are currently looking for other work, as discovered by Harvard and Stanford researchers who studied more than 17,000 employees in nineteen industries. When I first saw this number, I was terrified. I imagined 71 percent of our staff walking out the door on any given day. It would destroy us. Although I knew they wouldn't all leave together, I decided we must take action to encourage them to stay. We had, after all, made promises to these people. When you hire someone, they are likely dissatisfied with their last job, and you promise them something better. You must live up to that promise, as they have far more choice in where to work than you have great employees to choose from. There are also plenty of opportunities for employees to search for better places to work. People are no longer grabbing the classifieds, circling some jobs, and making calls. In this age of instant gratification, they can seek out new positions in any industry with just a few clicks. Glassdoor, Indeed, Monster, ZipRecruiter, and LinkedIn are just some of the platforms ready to help them find a new employer, or for prospective poachers to approach them. Even Google has entered the job-hunting market. Now, people will be served with ads for new jobs just like ads for vacuum cleaners or sunglasses.

Culture is what will keep employees. A cultured, values-driven approach to business is the only thing that can attract and retain great employees. They'll stay if they know the company is dedicated to matching their career goals and personal development, and if they feel part of a mission. Few places invest in their culture, so this is your advantage in becoming a more attractive workplace than those competing for your employees.

Finally, the power of the wrong person extends to operations. In his book *Good to Great: Why Some Companies Make the Leap...and Others Don't,* Jim Collins talks about the company leader with a thousand helpers, where no one is truly trained to do anything on their own. No one has the ability to manage a project on their own or run a department. Employees walk into the company owner's office and ask a question. They execute based on the answer, then go back to the owner and ask another question. This cycle repeats, and the owner cannot walk away or shift their focus from their employees' immediate problems. This is true hell. A company like this can never scale and it will always need the leader at the helm.

When you've hired the wrong people into your firm, no cultural initiatives can combat this. You will always have employees who refuse to think for themselves. You'll have a company of a thousand helpers. Conversely, when the right people are in place and supported by a mission and values driven culture, they will learn how to do their work without constant supervision. They will work hard, fail at times, discuss challenges, be open to coaching, and want themselves and the company to grow.

THE RIGHT PEOPLE

To avoid becoming or remaining a company of a thousand helpers, you must first hire the right people. Surround yourself with those who can help the firm succeed—people who are truly better than you. This is the most important area your firm can focus on, as there is no culture without great people. Great people are those who are disciplined, share your values, and are self-motivated. They have character and grit and positivity. Their skills are transferable, and they are open-minded enough to change. They have a desire to grow. We'll delve into these traits more in a moment, but finding them requires looking for those who are better than you. Few companies do this. We certainly didn't. As a result, we had an intense amount of turnover, which hurt our growth.

In *The Laws of Human Nature*, Robert Greene wrote, "If people are essentially lazy or foolish, they leave clues to this in the smallest of details that you can pick up well before their behavior harms you. The ability to gauge people's true worth, the degree of loyalty and conscientiousness, is one of the most important skills that you can possess, helping you avoid the bad hires, partnerships, and relationships that can make your life miserable."

With reading, research, and practice, we learned to pick up on the small details that reveal a person's true worth. Then, we found ourselves the right people.

MATCH YOUR VALUES

Recently, we were interviewing for a new case manager. As we've grown into a larger firm, department directors and managers now conduct interviews for their own team members. When I can, I stop by in-person interviews to offer support and see how they're going. As I joined the case manager interview, I thought the candidate, who we'll call Maria, seemed great. She came across as smart, well-dressed, professional, and direct. I was confident she could handle the job, as she'd come through our new hiring process. As we'll discuss below, that ensures an ability match, so the in-person interview is to determine if there is a cultural and values fit.

Ruben, our case management director, was conducting the interview. With each answer Maria gave, he gently pried for more information using two simple prompts: "Tell me more," and "Describe..." As he elicited more information, it became clear that Maria was not a good fit. She said she once had to send flowers to another employee as an apology. Our interest was piqued. When Ruben asked her to *tell us more,* she said she's been told she lacks empathy and is too direct. This concerned us, as empathy is one of our firm's core values. Ruben asked again, "Tell us more." Maria told us a story that demonstrated this trait.

At the time, she managed substitute teachers for a local school district. There was a teacher who failed to turn in her weekly reports. Maria met with her to explain that they must be completed. The teacher said she was having some issues outside of work but would get the reports done. Maria said she was direct with the teacher and reiterated the importance of the reports. It was clear that Maria saw her directness as a desirable trait for a law firm. It was also clear that she wasn't telling us the whole story. The conversation she described didn't explain why she had to send apology flowers to another employee. So, again, Ruben asked a simple question: "Can you describe the situation a bit more?"

Maria went on to explain that a week later, the teacher still had not turned in the reports. She arranged another meeting, in which the teacher began to cry, explaining that her father, who she cared for, had late-stage cancer and was going through a very difficult time. Without acknowledging the teacher's difficult situation, Maria said, "Well, are you going to get the job done, or do we have to find someone else who will?" As she recounted this conversation to us, Maria seemed to beam with some pride. It was clear she valued a harsh and direct approach to her job and thought this was a benefit in a law firm. We did not make an offer.

We are trying to build a place where people not only understand our values but live into them. Those values include acting with empathy, being vulnerable, fostering team and community, and working to better ourselves. Maria didn't value empathy, and she would have struggled to live into it. She would have had a tough time being vulnerable and prioritizing team and community. She had the best resume but wasn't the best match. A skillset or years of experience does not matter as much as matching values.

Our annual employee-of-the-year accolade is The Foxhole Award. It goes to the person who most embodies our values and helps their fellow teammates. When taking nominations for the award, we ask, "Who would you most want to be in the foxhole with?" When we hire, no matter the position, we look for potential Foxhole Award winners. We search for people who want to contribute beyond a paycheck, who will help their teammates, cover when others are out, and care for everything at the highest level because that is just in their nature.

VALUES CRAFT CHARACTER

A person's values craft their character. When hiring, we

worry less about a candidate's hard skills, such as whether they're a good personal injury paralegal, and more about their character. Hard skills and knowledge can be taught. Character cannot.

Angela Duckworth, a social psychologist and the author of the bestselling book *Grit,* makes the case that grit is the most significant character trait in any successful person. She defines grit as perseverance and passion for long-term goals. A person with grit sticks things out, follows up, refuses to quit, and shows stamina. Duckworth argues these are not traits we are born with. Grit starts developing at a young age and is generally taught by a parent, teacher, or coach. She says a demanding and supportive environment is required to raise gritty children. The same is true to create a company of gritty characters. Leaders and managers demand great work from their colleagues and are there to support their struggle.

The best people for this environment are those who already have character. They were raised to embody grit and can help promote it in others. However, some people have never experienced a strong, supportive, and demanding home or company. It's difficult to know if they will rise to the occasion and display grit when needed, but there are a few indicators that suggest they will respond well. Playing on a sports team, participating in a debate team, being a former military member, or accomplishing something special all suggest the person in question can overcome obstacles in a demanding and supportive environment and has or is capable of developing grit. If you pair these people with a principled company, a great mission, and values, the team will soar. Duckworth explains this with a simple example: Three bricklayers are asked, "What are you doing?" The first says, "I'm laying bricks." The second says, "I'm building a church." And the third says, "I'm building the house of God." The first bricklayer has a job; the second has a career; the third has a calling.

Grit is like Daniel H. Pink's description of buoyancy. In Pink's book *To Sell Is Human: The Surprising Truth about Moving Others*, he argues that everybody in a modern company is a salesperson. After all, sales *is* motivation. In any position, motivating others has become a large and consistent part of the job. Traditionally, salespeople lived by the maxim of ABC: Always Be Closing. The mindset was one of continually pushing to close the deal. Pink argues that successful, modern businesspeople, all of whom are in sales in some way, have to replace that idea with a new ABC: Attunement, Buoyancy, and Clarity.

Attunement is about being able to read people and situations, anticipating what's coming. It's being able to stay in touch with your existing culture at any given time, so you can sense issues before they become problematic, as we discussed in chapter three.

Recently, Bilal and I had dinner in San Francisco with the legendary trial lawyer Bill Veen and his head trial counsel Anthony Label. We didn't have much time for dinner and had quite a bit to discuss. San Francisco is known for its restaurants and often for the overcomplication of its food. When he delivered our first course, the waiter carefully put down our dishes and then explained in excruciating detail the ingredients, where they came from, how they were prepared, and how this differed from traditional preparation methods. He repeated this with eight different dishes! It ate up our precious time. The waiter was clearly so proud of the food that he couldn't become *attuned* to what our table wanted, which was to be left to our conversation.

Buoyancy is the ability to bounce back from the setbacks that happen each day. It's the positive attitude required to pick yourself up and keep moving. It's the grit that Angela Duckworth talks about, and the ability to handle the daily curveballs. Buoyancy keeps people afloat as they pursue long-term goals. The challenges of owning a law firm can sometimes feel like getting kicked in the teeth twenty times a day. Buoyancy lets you shrug off the abuse, smile, and move onto the next task. A buoyant person is, more often than not, successful.

I recently heard Hal Elrod speak. Elrod is the author of *The Morning Miracle: The Not-So-Obvious Secret Guaran-*

teed to Transform Your Life (Before 8AM), a book on the importance of a morning ritual. He learned buoyancy from his first boss, who taught him "the five-minute rule." When something negative happens, you set a timer. You're allowed to be negative for five minutes. After five minutes is up, you move on. Elrod is sincere in his use of this. After an almost-deadly car accident and a battle with cancer, he said the five-minute rule forced him to be positive no matter the severity of the situation.

Clarity is the ability to be more knowledgeable than your clients and to communicate that knowledge effectively to them. In today's world, knowledge is everywhere, but it is not always good knowledge. Often, prospects and clients believe they know all about the law and process because *they read it on the internet.* And of course, everything we read on the internet is true! To manage this, we must have as much *true* knowledge about our jobs as possible. Employees with character will be there to learn, grow, and help. That means they'll be willing to learn their job so well that they can effectively communicate with even the most "knowledgeable" clients.

POSITIVE PEOPLE

Buoyant people have a positive life perspective, and that's what you're looking for. We're not talking about those sickeningly upbeat life coaches and yoga/meditation instructors who live on a beach and spout quotes about the positivity of the universe. In a law firm, you just need good, solid, happy people who look for the best in any situation.

There are several ways to spot a positive or negative attitude in an interview. You can sometimes see it in a candidate's face. Naturally, they're putting their best foot forward in an interview, but they struggle to keep the light expression of a more positive person. Mostly, you want to listen. You can hear the attitude in how they talk about previous jobs. A positive person will find something useful in any experience. Even if their last place was terrible, they'll say, "You know, I made some nice friends there," or "I learned a lot." If a candidate says, "I couldn't stand my last job. They gave us too much work. We were overwhelmed. Blah, blah, blah," it signals they're stuck on the negative and unable to see any benefits of a situation.

A positive person will always find a good side. Negative people are down about everything. Their commute is too long. Their office chair doesn't work properly. Their desk is too tall or too short or too small. They can't stop complaining. When you fix their chair, they complain about the castor wheels. When you loosen up the wheels, they bitch about the carpet.

As the Papa John's story shows, one bad person can kill

a company. They can destroy everything you've built. In our firm, we haven't experienced full destruction, but negative people have certainly damaged us. One of our former assistants, a wonderful young woman and a graduate of the University of California, Berkeley, quit because she couldn't stand the negativity of her case manager. Positive people can't be around negativity, and the case manager constantly spewed negativity. When I closed my office door, she told people I must be talking about her. She was skilled, but the negativity affected her work to the extent that we had to let her go. We lost a great employee for a negative one, who we ended up losing anyway. Practical skills never trump negativity.

It's important to note that *negative* is not a synonym for *unlikeable*. We recently had an employee I liked very much. Henry was smart and studied psychology in college. He'd read all the great writers and we had some inspiring conversations about them. Unfortunately, he was also extraordinarily angry and cynical. He had a very fixed mindset, viewing his circumstances as unmovable and hopeless. He was from an immigrant family and saw his life prospects as limited. He often said that only people from privilege could succeed. No matter how much we talked, he couldn't see another side to this. I knew this attitude would be his biggest challenge. Henry was still young, only just out of college, and I wanted to help him overcome this hurdle before it became more deeply engrained. We had many conversations, and his attitude started to improve, but I sensed he still thought he was better than the job.

We work daily with a local vendor whose service is essential in keeping our cases moving along. One day, Henry got into an argument on the phone with someone at the vendor's office. I don't know what triggered it, but he got angry. Following the call, he sent a fax to the person he argued with and scrawled across the top of the page, "You're rude. You should go to charm school." It turned out that the person he spoke to was the owner of the company. The owner called Bilal to discuss the situation, and politely said that Henry was never allowed to call their office again. This vendor is extremely important to our firm and communicating with them was a core function of Henry's position. Thankfully, Bilal knew the company's owner well and was able to apologize. He smoothed the whole thing over. However, were it not for Bilal's people skills, Henry's negative attitude might have cost us a critical partner. We had to let Henry go. Amazingly enough, even after getting fired, Henry insisted his behavior was okay. Such is the strength of a negative mindset in someone unwilling to change.

HIRE FOR SOFT SKILLS

"You hire for hard skills and fire for soft skills." That's

the old saying that acts as a warning for everyone who scans resumes for tangible skills and neglects to assess soft skills such as positivity. We hired Henry through our old, unconscious process. He appeared to have strong hard skills and, back then, we didn't know to evaluate a person's soft skillset. A candidate may have the hard skills of, say, legal knowledge, but the soft skills are more important. These are the traits that cannot be taught. In subsequent years, we've learned that character traits carry through from industry to industry, position to position. Bank tellers do well in our firm. They may have never seen workers' compensation before, but they're well-trained with a solid understanding of process and procedure. If they are motivated, smart, positive, happy, and gritty, we will hire someone like that any day.

Your core team must have transferable soft skills that can adapt as your business grows and pivots. If you only hire for skills required by the current job, how will your staff pivot to something new? The ability to pivot will keep you afloat when the world around you changes. In 2011, I shifted into workers' compensation for athletes because the financial markets crashed. My entertainment and athlete clients stopped doing business deals, real estate deals, and buying and selling businesses. They rarely wanted to go through with expensive litigation. That work dried up, and I had to figure out something new.

In 2013, I had to pivot again. That year, the California legislature passed a law cutting the legs out from athlete workers' compensation. Before that, the California Workers' Compensation system was one of the few places where retired NFL players and other athletes could get compensation for injuries they suffered throughout their career. This was also around the time when concussion issues were finally starting to surface. These athletes have huge problems with chronic traumatic encephalopathy (CTE) and brain disease. For many years, California allowed most people who played team sports, regardless of where they played, to file cases in California. Average payouts in these cases were far higher than those of regular compensation cases. However, with CTE cases coming to the forefront, the NFL lobbied for new rules which would shut down most of the athlete cases in California. They were successful, and when those rules came into effect, my pool of potential clients dropped by about 75 percent.

That's when we pivoted to practicing community-based workers' compensation, which is quite a different area of law. It requires a separate knowledge base and different skills. It was at this time that Bilal joined me. He had the experience in community-based workers' comp that I lacked. Other people in the company didn't have the ability to pivot and we had to let several of them go. Bilal has proved to be an excellent partner and a huge reason for our success. I also know the team we have now is resilient and adaptable. If we have to pivot again, we will.

THE DESIRE TO GROW

If you want your firm to grow, you must surround yourself with people willing to grow personally and professionally with you. They must be able to transfer their skills from one area to another as you pivot and expand. In the beginning, they will need to be jacks of all trades, even willing to clean the kitchen and take out the trash. When you know what they're best at, you can put them in charge of that thing. If they're willing to grow, they'll master that position, and then you'll find them a new one.

Colleen Barrett is an excellent example of an employee willing to grow. She graduated from Becker Junior College in 1964 and worked for several years as an executive assistant at a law firm. The firm was owned by Herb Kelleher, who was the lawyer for Southwest Airlines. Eventually, Herb joined Southwest as a full-time employee and later became their chief executive officer. Barrett moved to Southwest with Kelleher and was his assistant there. She stayed the course, applied her transferable skills to this new industry, and showed incredible grit. She was promoted over the years and moved through the ranks, becoming vice-president and finally president of the airline. Barrett is credited with some of the amazing innovations that have made Southwest Airlines one of the few profitable airlines in history. After a successful stint, she is now their president emeritus and corporate secretary.

Barrett had transferable, soft skills, and was willing to work hard, and her desire to grow, adapt, and thrive was embraced by Southwest Airlines' culture. That culture encouraged and empowered Barrett. This could not have happened in a typical organization; Southwest is perennially named one of the best places to work. In 2019, it placed in Glassdoor's top ten best workplaces. You can translate "great place to work" as "a place of great culture." Great cultures develop legal secretaries into presidents of legendary companies.

The receptionists you walk past each day, the person in the mailroom, and the assistants to attorneys are all incredible people who can grow your organization exponentially. Your job is to care for and develop these people. Treat them well. Fulfill and then exceed their basic human needs. Create a demanding, disciplined, and supportive environment led by its values. Reward their positivity and apply their soft skills wherever they are needed. Get these good people into the right seats, regardless of whether they hold the "required" hard skills. In return, they will give you their all. They will stick around and grow from one position to another within your firm, feeling like the company matches their career goals at every stage. In the next section, we'll take a deep dive into a hiring process that helps you discover these superstars.

CHAPTER SEVEN

DELIBERATE AND CONSCIENTIOUS HIRING

"Hiring people is an art, not a science, and resumes can't tell you whether someone will fit into a company's culture."

—HOWARD SCHULTZ

A while ago, we interviewed an attorney with great skills. We'd already worked with him on many cases and knew he was an excellent defense lawyer. He was also a slob. He often showed up at our office for depositions and other meetings in a crumpled T-shirt. When we took him for a meal, he ordered a cheeseburger and fries, and boy did he attack his plate. He ripped the burger apart with his fingers, smashed the chunks into ketchup, and smeared grease everywhere. I found myself shifting away to avoid the splash zone. I thought, *How the hell can I ever take this guy to a charity event?*

We, on the other hand, like to look professional. We ask our people to dress well and use good manners. We expect them to be polite. We interviewed this guy because he had a decent reputation in the community, and his skills would likely have been a good addition to our team. It was clear, though, that he didn't share our professional values. But here's the shameful truth: we still offered him a job. There are so few lawyers out there in our sector of the industry, and we were desperate. The work was stacking up, and the team was struggling. We had yet to employ our new hiring practices, which I'll detail in this chapter, and we fell victim to hiring in desperation.

Thankfully, he turned the offer down. I don't know why. Perhaps he sensed we weren't a good fit and was smart enough to listen to the warning signs. Later, I reflected on our good luck. This guy's table manners were likely indicative of how he practiced law: fast, furious, and messy. He may have had a good reputation, but I am always wary of disorganization. He wouldn't have matched our style.

A GOOD MUTUAL FIT

Every resume includes the same old inflated experiences and impressive phrases. You have to read resumes very carefully and look between the lines to find the right people. The resume is a marketing document. It is supposed to present a person in their best light, yet it is amazing how many people submit resumes with typos! No matter how strong the resume might be, we are now disciplined. When we see typos, we pass it by.

This isn't easy when everyone's telling you how amazing they are, so it requires a deliberate and conscientious process to weed people out. This process should extend from posting a job vacancy to conducting telephone interviews, running in-person interviews, testing, checking references, and onboarding successful candidates. Many big companies have adopted a hiring process; getting a job at Google takes months. Most small- to mid-sized law firms, however, are stuck in desperation hiring. They're so impatient to get someone in that they look for a few skills, make sure the candidate is kind of nice, offer the lowest wage they can, and get them started. They feel their way through hiring without applying much process.

Adam Robinson outlines a solid process to vet the right people for your firm in his book, *The Best Team Wins: Build Your Business Through Predictive Hiring*. His method of reducing a stack of resumes to just a handful for interviews, three to five at most, has been a game changer for our firm. We read about and implemented his process, which I recommend. Once we've narrowed the field to a maximum of five candidates, we talk to them. I don't mean we ask an assistant to call them in. Rather, one of our best employees conducts a very scripted telephone interview for about forty-five minutes. Much of our process is based on Robinson's book, however there are many great methods of getting the right people in the door. We chose Robinson's method, in part, because of Hireology, his company's applicant tracking system, which is based on the process outlined in the book. This system makes it easy to implement Robinson's hiring philosophy. Regardless of which method you choose, find a system that works for your firm.

If you're a solo practitioner or run a small firm of, say, less than thirty people, you are still building your core team, and you should probably run the hiring process yourself to ensure each new person truly matches your needs. Once you have mastered deliberate and conscientious hiring through your chosen method, you can teach the system to others. If you have a larger team, you may have delegated hiring to a human resources person and department heads. If so, make sure they are trained! We had each person involved in hiring read Robinson's book to better understand the philosophy behind the process.

Take care in choosing who to train in this skill. Hiring the right people is not only the most important thing you do, but it is nuanced and difficult, so only your best should be involved. Great people want to work with other great people. They seek out coworkers who will make them better. Mediocre employees don't want great coworkers. Accomplished people will make them look bad, so they seek out mediocre people to join the team. Don't let that happen.

The process starts with digging deep when you create a job listing. That means you must understand the core skills, both hard and soft, required for each position within your company. When we transitioned to this new process, we worked hard to ensure our job descriptions encompassed the *entire* job. We already discussed the importance of soft skills such as positivity and a willingness to learn and grow. For us, the required soft skills are essentially the same for every position, with a few minor, nuanced changes. We include these in the job listing along with the necessary hard skills and share the advertisement through several placement sites. When we receive a resume we like, we send a copy of the job description to the candidate via email along with a link to an interview calendar. The email says something like this:

> Thank you for contacting us. We are impressed with your resume and would love to learn more about you. Attached is a current job description for the position to which you have applied. Please review it and, if you are still interested in the position, click the calendar link and book an appointment for an initial phone interview.

Between the job post, which also includes a great deal of

information on the company, and the job description, the candidate knows a lot about what they're getting into. If they move forward, we don't have to spend much time explaining about the company and the job. We also place responsibility on them to book the appointment. Hiring is a long process that can take several weeks, so we try to group the phone interviews together. They can be intense, so we limit them to three per day. We manage this using the availability settings on the calendar. Our goal is to conduct phone interviews with about ten to fifteen candidates and invite three to five of them to in-person interviews. We've found we need about fifty to seventy-five resumes to find this number of potential candidates for the next step.

When we call a candidate, we run through a series of scripted, high-level questions. The scripts are almost identical for every position, regardless of whether the candidate is applying to be an attorney or a receptionist. The only variation is in a small, customized section that relates to basic daily duties. We let the candidates know the questions are preplanned. We explain we have a long and deliberate recruitment process that includes regimented scripts, so we can be certain every candidate is asked the same questions and is given an even playing field in which to respond. We know they will talk about their various achievements and responsibilities, and we'll get an idea of their skills. The questions are designed to give us an idea of their long- and short-term career goals, their current skills, and their previous positions. We are also very clear about the position. We try to get a sense of what people like to do every day and whether those wants will match the job.

I recall one candidate who we thought would be a wonderful fit for the case management department. As we went through the questions, I liked her more and more. Finally, we got to the question about what they *don't* like to do every day. Her response was deflating. She said she hated talking on the phone with clients. She liked clients and felt she was good at communicating, but really disliked being on the phone for large periods of time. Well, that was an immediate deal breaker. Our case managers and assistant case managers spend six hours a day or more on the phone. We explained this, and we both agreed the position wasn't a good mutual fit. We don't try to oversell a position to a candidate or convince them this experience will be different. If a core function of the job is to talk on the phone and the person doesn't like that, it's best to figure this out *before* you hire them. This process is designed to find people who can enjoy being at the company a long time.

As candidates talk, the most critical follow-ups are simple: "Tell me more," and, "Describe..." The more they describe, the better sense we get of their values, character, positivity, and desire to grow. We're also able to pick up on red flags, such as how they talk about their previous company. One of my favorite questions is in the section on previous jobs. We ask, "Are you still in touch with your previous supervisor?" You can tell a lot from this answer. Professionals generally remain in touch with their former leaders. This is true at our company. The former rock-star employees are those who, despite leaving for various reasons, are still in touch with us. We call them PWC Alumni and invite them to all of our events. They may have left because of life changes or for jobs closer to home, but they all left on good terms and are still part of our family. When candidates tell us they've been to their supervisor's home, they still text with them, ask them for job advice, and so on, we feel confident they are a candidate with great character.

The last important aspect of the phone interview is the opportunity to explore down the road. We are a firm that promises growth, so we want to ensure that what we can offer in the long-term matches the candidate's life goals. To do this, we ask a series of questions about the future, such as, "What would you like to have accomplished in your career in twenty years?" Really good people can envision this. We interviewed a marketing director who said, "I want to have a significant impact on building brands." She had the forethought to consider what truly interested her and would satisfy her career. Even when someone applies for a junior position, I want to see they've put some thought into their future. I want to know they're motivated to do more than just sit in a cubicle.

By the time they're invited to an in-person interview, we know they are professionals who want the job and are a good mutual fit. The in-person interview lasts for three-and-a-half hours or more. It starts with cognitive and psychological testing through Hireology. There are many good testing systems out there. Find one you like and use it. After completing the tests, candidates meet with two people, usually the department director and a department manager. These leaders interview for their team members, as they are best positioned to determine who is the best fit. As our firm has grown, we've created micro-groups of three to five employees, and each group adopts its own identity within the larger culture. A recruit must be a cultural fit with the firm *and* the micro-group.

This is the interview's main purpose: to determine a cultural fit. Do this candidate's values match ours? Do they want to work in our style? Is this someone you'd want to have a beer with? We ask scripted open-ended questions, and let the candidate talk until we answer the underlying issue of whether they're a cultural fit. We're also listening for soft skills indicators. What is their time management process? Are they motivated? Do they care about meeting deadlines? What is their method for problem-solving?

We're not asking about the knowledge required for this job. We're inquiring about life skills necessary for *any* position. As lawyers, we know how to ask open-ended questions like this, and we should be applying this skill to our hiring process.

THE REFERENCE CHECK

Many years ago, I had a law clerk named Gil who worked for me during his tenure in law school. He was only with me for a short time before going on to great things. We've remained good friends, and he was actually the catalyst and encouragement for my entering into our current business. He has a workers' compensation law firm in Newport Beach, California, which is very similar to ours. Several months before I even secured Bilal as our first attorney, when I was about to pivot into the same area of law, I visited Gil in his office. We sat around his desk, and I shared my concerns about my new venture.

"I can't do this alone," I said, "and I don't have anyone who knows how to do community-based workers' comp."

"Oh, one of our guys is about to move to San Francisco. Maybe he'll work for you." With that, Gil hit his speakerphone and called out, "Hey, Irving, come into my office." Irving walked in and sat down next to me. He was a well-dressed guy in his mid-twenties. Gil said to Irving,

"You're going to law school in San Francisco, right? Are you doing night classes or day?"

"Night," said Irving.

"Do you need a job during the day?"

"Yeah."

"Great, you can work for Eric." Gil looked at me and said, "That's okay, right?"

"Sure," I said. And that's how I hired Irving.

Irving runs operations now and helps Bilal and me run the company. He joined as a legal assistant, was an excellent employee, and worked his way up to director of operations. He oversees the operations of the entire firm and allows me to take breaks for close to four weeks at a time, which is unheard of for most law firm owners. Clearly, Irving didn't come in through our current, detailed hiring process. In many ways, we got lucky in finding him. Really, though, Irving came to us through a very relaxed reference check. Gil is a trusted friend, and he recommended Irving to us. A reference check is a recommendation.

If someone has had a previous job, and we now only hire those who have, you need to get on the phone with their former supervisor. With good people, this generally isn't a problem. They tend to become friends with their coworkers and supervisors. They stay in touch with them and care about their professional development. When we made our very first hire through our new, deliberative process, I was still managing recruitment myself. We were interviewing a woman and things were going great. I got on the phone with her previous boss, who said, "Oh, yeah, I talk to her all the time. She's fantastic. I wish she'd been able to stay with us, but life was moving on, and she was developing into greater things." Then she said, "Look, you'd be an idiot not to hire her." So we hired her.

You're looking for references like that. You want to hear glowing reviews that can't possibly be fake. I once called a bank with a policy against giving out references. The candidate's former supervisor said, "We're not allowed to talk about previous employees, but here's my cell number. Call me after hours." I did, and she gushed about the candidate. She genuinely wanted to help this person out. She offered real praise. There was none of that "Yes, she was fine to work with" bullshit. This matters whether you're hiring attorneys, assistants, or staff for the mailroom. Every position requires a professional. You can only determine someone's professionalism by speaking to their former employer.

So many companies skip this step. They can't get hold of

the reference the first time, and they don't worry about following up. They think, *Oh, this person seemed nice. I'm sure it'll be fine.* Getting a good reference for a good person should be a simple affair. If it's not, something is wrong. Professionals remain in touch with their former supervisors. They become friends, attend their life events, birthdays, weddings, and so on. This has been a common experience with our own people. We're still in touch with all our best people, even years after they've left. We call them our alumni, and they are some of the biggest champions of our firm in the community.

LET THE SEAT SIT EMPTY

Resist the pressure to fill a seat with the wrong person. If the right person isn't in your pool of candidates, bide your time. Get outside help. Go to a temp agency, if you must, but do not hire the wrong person. If you have a team, this is when you ask them to step up and fill the gap. When you already have the right people in the right seats, they'll rally around and ensure the work gets done. We had a micro-team who, for a while, was missing its third person—the assistant. We told the other two team members, "Look, we're going to find you someone as soon as possible, but we don't want to hire you the wrong person." Those two team members met more often, got better organized and more in sync, and still met their goals, even with one-third of their team absent. In fact, they crushed it and came close to doubling their goals during that period. It took time, but we got the right person for the team, and they continue to thrive.

Whether we got ten resumes or one hundred for a vacancy, we would hire the best person in that candidate pool. This is a terrible way to operate. The new hire might have had the skills to get the job done, but they didn't necessarily share our values. Otherwise, they would share our values and be completely incompetent. They could be a slob with no professionalism or a manager who lacked empathy. These days, we don't just grab the best person in a candidate pool. We wait for the right person.

It takes courage to trust the process, but, no matter what, you must let the seat sit empty until you find the right person. You don't have any fucking excuses. I hear from people across the country that they can't find the right people. Our area has a 2 percent unemployment rate, and we can wait for the right person. So, I don't want to hear your excuses for why this can't be done. Be patient, be deliberate, and hire conscientiously.

A WORD ABOUT MILLENNIALS

I used to be very awkward around millennials. We have had many work for us, and we still do. At first they just looked like clock-watching phone zombies to me. They seemed more concerned with lunchtime and running out of the office at 5 p.m. than with working hard. I often struggled to talk to them. This was a challenging experience for me, as I can usually talk to anybody. I recall being so uncomfortable standing in the kitchen with one of our millennials, pouring myself a coffee while they made avocado toast. I didn't know what to talk to them about. I just couldn't relate to someone who had never seen *Seinfeld*.

Then we hired Lauren. She was a millennial and she was just wonderful. Lauren was one of our early employees and came to us straight out of school. She is smart, calm, soft-spoken, compassionate, and caring. We finally had a millennial I really liked. One day, she was getting up from her desk, ready to head home for the evening. I said, "Lauren, can I talk to you for a minute?" She looked at me and said, "It's after 5 p.m." Then she gave me a half-apologetic smile and left the office. I couldn't believe it. *Are you kidding?* I thought. It was three minutes after five, I was her boss, and I wanted to speak for one minute. I couldn't understand her mindset. Lauren wasn't an asshole; she was smart and kind. She cared about our clients and the work. She was the type of person I wanted working for us—in every aspect except for this. After my indignation wore off, I wondered how I could keep Lauren motivated at work. I wanted her to remain engaged, and, if possible, prevent my head from exploding when she waltzed out at 5 p.m. on the dot.

I was also aware that Lauren was not an isolated issue. Millennials make up 35 percent of the general workforce and it will not be long before they are the majority. This felt like bad news. Aside from my personal awkwardness around them, millennials have a bad reputation. The media and most older people—including me—have stereotyped them as lazy clock-watchers who don't care enough about anything. Some millennials even believe this of themselves. When criticized for slacking off or being distracted, they'll say, "Well, I'm a millennial. That's how I'm supposed to be." This reputation causes many people of my generation to be hesitant in hiring them. But times were changing, and I knew I'd be in trouble if I couldn't figure out how to get people like Lauren to stick around.

I read all I could about millennials. I discovered that most, if not all, are concerned citizens who want to make a positive impact on the world. They are purpose-driven. This means there's a new generation of lawyers and staff who want to be more humanistic. If your firm has a purpose-driven culture that puts human needs first and lives by a set of values, millennials will embrace that. It will help them feel empowered to positively impact the world in a bigger way than they could ever accomplish alone.

They also want to stop and smell the roses and take vacations. They don't let work become their everything.

Rather, they want it to be a driving force for a healthy life. Everybody could do with more of that attitude. So many professionals in my generation work too much. There are so many benefits to rest and relaxation. I spent most of my career thinking there was too much to do right now; I could take a break next week. Next week would come, and the break would not. In many ways, that's what led to my back collapsing and my mind burning out.

My research led to a revelation about another seemingly negative millennial stereotype. The statistics say millennials jump around in their jobs. They won't stay put, and they have no loyalty. When I dug deep into the analysis, though, I discovered that millennials do value stability. They simply won't stay loyal to a company without a stable, purpose-driven culture. They'll jump ship to find a more secure situation, and they won't feel bad about it. This is understandable when you consider what they've witnessed. During the Great Recession, which started in late 2007, they watched their parents' jobs disappear after decades of service. They saw houses lost, retirement accounts destroyed, and families sunk. For most millennials, this created a deep disdain for big, heartless companies.

I *want* employees who care about their impact on the world. I want people who prioritize their health to prevent burnout. And I respect those who are unwilling to sacrifice their stability to a big, heartless company. Millennials, it turns out, are people I want to be around. They care about the greater good more than any other generation. They want to save the environment and contribute to society's success. They're conscious of the food they eat—perhaps more than necessary. They're mindful. They care about the things that make us human. They bring their whole selves to work. I'll take that over *Seinfeld* any day.

I also realized that millennials are no different from any other generation in the workforce. There are plenty of unmotivated forty-, fifty-, and sixty-year-olds out there watching the clock, avoiding the difficult work, and heading out exactly at 5 p.m!

I began to embrace our millennials. I tried to make them feel cared for, so they'd want to stay with our firm. I wanted to create a culture that would keep these hard-working, conscientious people around. In many ways, this led me down a rabbit hole of cultural improvements, which resulted in millennials staying loyal to the firm, and older staff improving their work *and* their lives. We created a more age-diverse workplace. Many studies prove diverse environments are more creative and innovative than homogeneous ones. With our improved age diversity, we became a more creative company. Greater creativity led to less turnover and more profits. It all contributed to our success.

Lauren, Irving, and our other millennials were certainly one of the catalysts for creating our purpose-driven culture. Lauren became one of the best employees we've had. When workloads were heavy, she stayed late and came in on weekends. There were few people in our company's history with such a natural ability to speak with clients. There were plenty of days she left right at 5 p.m., sometimes to teach English to new immigrants and other times to get certified as a yoga instructor. She ran our wellness program, arranging speakers and even leading some yoga classes for the staff. She left recently to travel the world with her boyfriend for a few years. When she told us she was leaving, she gave more than six months' notice to ensure a smooth transition. She is one of our PWC Alumni.

Do not shy away from hiring millennials. If you do not embrace them, you'll lack the diversity and creativity of your competitors. Eventually, the workforce will age out, and you will go out of business. Millennials are the future, for better or worse. From what I see, it will make the world—and its law firms—much, much better.

CHAPTER EIGHT

A LIFE EXPERIENCE

"How you do anything is how you do everything."

—RYAN HOLIDAY

Imagine James is starting a new job at an average mid-sized law firm. A few weeks ago, he signed the contract and was left to wonder what his first day would look like. When that day arrives, he walks into the firm's lobby and introduces himself to the receptionist.

"Hi, I'm James. I'm starting here today."

"Oh, nobody told me," says the receptionist, looking flustered. "Can you wait right here? What department are you in? I'll try to find someone." She bustles off, leaving James to sit and wait. Eventually, the receptionist sends him up to the human resources (HR) manager, who gets James to fill out a bunch of paperwork. Then, the HR manager walks him around the office, bombarding him with the names of people they pass.

"That's Robert," she says, waving at a man talking on a phone in a cubicle. Robert nods in acknowledgment. They arrive at James's desk, which has a monitor but no computer, and an unplugged phone. The IT guy hasn't had time to stop by and set things up. They eventually get all the cords plugged into the right places, and James is left to watch some training videos.

This is a typical first-day scenario in so many companies, and it's just lackluster. It squanders the emotional charge of starting a new job. It should be an exciting morning for James, but instead, it's full of awkward, half-hearted interactions. There's no feeling to it. It's dull, disorganized, and about as momentous as taking your car for a fucking oil change. This kind of experience is enough to make James question if he should have accepted the position. It might be so demoralizing that he goes home that evening, opens up his laptop, and starts scanning job search sites again.

In *The Power of Moments: Why Certain Experiences Have Extraordinary Impact,* authors Chip and Dan Heath drive home a concept we all know but easily forget: starting a new job is one of life's great moments. Most people place it within the top five important moments of their lives. It's up there along with turning twenty-one, graduating, getting married, and having a child. We have huge celebrations for these other life events. There are parties, ceremonies, wedding receptions, and new baby gift baskets.

Chip and Dan Heath teach that we should celebrate a new hire and give it the attention a top-five life experience deserves. It's an opportunity to harness a new employee's excitement, which helps them fully commit to and engage with the firm. Many studies show that an employee's engagement in their first ninety days is an excellent indicator of how long they'll stick around and how well they'll perform. Companies that properly engage employees from the outset experience less turnover. Those staff members perform better in the long term, and their companies have more success.

You create engagement through a culture that celebrates life events. The best way to celebrate is through a curated onboarding experience that starts the moment the employment agreement is signed and extends throughout an employee's first ninety days. We'll discuss what this looks like, but I first want you to understand that curating experiences in the initial period builds an enormous amount of trust. A new employee will be amazed when you quickly deliver on promises made during interviews. Our company has a mission to deliver world-class customer service to our clients *and also our team*. This service starts the moment they enter an interview.

Employers make a lot of promises in interview rooms. *We're a great place to work. We encourage a good work-life balance. We care about our staff.* Yet most of the time, they don't live up to the ideal they presented. Perhaps they have the best intentions, but they lack policies to support a work-life balance, or a caring attitude, or whatever they promised.

One of the most heartwarming compliments I ever received was from a receptionist, Karla, who you met in an earlier chapter. We hired Karla in our very early days. After a short time with us, she said, "I've never worked for a company that promised so much and lived up to every single thing." Since then, Karla has worked hard, cared for our clients, and made her way up the ranks. She's now our intake director responsible for designing the potential client experience, motivating our sales staff, overseeing the department, analyzing mounds of data, and keeping our law firm fed with new clients.

When you live up to the expectations set in the interview room, employees reciprocate. They deliver on all the promises they made regarding themselves: *I'm hardworking. I'm a good team player. I enjoy creative problem-solving.* All those bullshit interview clichés become real. They become the best version of themselves. You set a standard: this is a place where we live up to our promises. They internalize that message and fall in line. They work to please you. They get involved with the culture. They seek out more responsibilities and areas of growth. As they grow, so does the firm.

THE FIRST-DAY EXPERIENCE

Let's compare James's experience to a hypothetical new hire at our firm. By the time we offer Annie a job with us, we've already made deliberate efforts to curate her experience. We wrote a job posting that honestly reflected the position. When she initially applied, we directed her to a full job description and our company values statement. Her phone interview started on time. When she arrived for her in-person interview, a team member was waiting to greet her in the lobby. "Welcome, Annie. You're here for the interview. Here's an agenda showing what you'll be doing today. John will be here in a moment to take you through. Oh, I see him walking down already. Can I get you anything before you get started?" It created a moment for Annie. She felt like we cared about her. It was an initial experience filled with positivity, thoughtfulness, and momentum.

Her interviewer John walked Annie to a conference room where a sign on the door read, *New Hire Interview, Annie*

Smith. There was water on the table, and John fetched her a coffee. We say we care for people, so the least we can do is get them a fucking coffee when they arrive. The coffee, agenda, and other small, deliberate actions accumulated to create the impression that we do things properly here.

After a successful interview and background and reference checks, Annie accepts our job offer through our electronic onboarding system. Then she starts hearing from our team. Our mentorship director emails her the day after she accepts the position. He introduces himself, gives her details of her mentor's name and experience with the firm, and asks her T-shirt size. He informs Annie that her mentor will take her to lunch on her first day, and he asks what kind of food she likes. The questions start a conversation, which helps Annie engage with the team before she even starts. A few days later, Annie's department director emails her. She welcomes her to the team, provides her cell phone number, and asks if Annie has any questions. She tells Annie where to park on her first day, what the dress code is, and when we expect her. Annie immediately feels connected to the group.

When that first day comes, Annie's mentor is waiting in the lobby for her. He walks her from the entrance to her desk, which is decorated. There's a welcome card signed by the entire team, a personalized note from me and my partner, and a swag bag containing pens, a water bottle, a

T-shirt, and a polo shirt. Propped on her desk is a framed certificate for Future Employee of the Year and a full-color book on our company culture. There's also a letter from our human resources manager inviting Annie to briefly review the materials on the desk and come to his office at 9:30 a.m. The screen saver on the computer says, "Welcome to the most important job you will ever have!"

Shortly before that time, Annie's mentor arrives to accompany her to HR. He walks Annie through the office but does *not* introduce her to anyone along the way. In other places, new hires are often shown around by someone gesturing vaguely toward busy employees who barely look up from their screens. We want to maintain Annie's excitement for her new job, and those half-hearted interactions are a sure way of flattening that energy. Instead, we have a rule that Annie's mentor can only introduce her to people who are up from their desks. When someone walks down the hall toward them, Annie's mentor stops and introduces her. When they walk past people in their cubicles, they don't stop. Annie can meet those people later when they have time to give her the welcome she deserves.

This flips the script on James's experience. We account for almost every minute of Annie's first day. Unlike James, she goes home, sits at the dinner table, and raves about her first day. "It's such a great place," she tells her partner. "I'm sure I'll get more substance tomorrow, but oh, man, I really like these people." That's what you want new hires saying after their first day. It's so much better than wondering if they made the right choice.

EXTENDING THE EXCITEMENT

We use rituals to extend a new employee's excitement as we acclimate them to our culture. If this sounds a little cultish, consider the word *culture*. It starts with cult, and rituals are an integral part of cult behavior. Robert Greene speaks to this in his best-selling book *The 48 Laws of Power*, which was declared a "mega cult classic" by *Fast Company*. Greene says rituals serve to bring every member in sync with the cult. We've deliberately designed rituals that align new employees with our cultural expectations. These include The 30-Day Email, The Failure Log, and CANI: Constant and Never-Ending Improvement program.

We discussed The 30-Day Email in chapter three when we looked at gratitude. We've been experimenting with having new employees end their day by emailing their direct supervisor. In that message, they detail what they accomplished that day, the questions that arose, and any challenges they encountered. They end the email by dedicating the next day to someone meaningful in their life, which prompts them to express gratitude.

The CANI program is based on the Japanese philosophy of kaizen, which means constant improvement. Toyota, now the world's largest automaker, credits kaizen for increasing its business. At Toyota, kaizen means all employees are tasked with finding problems that the company can improve upon. Everyone, from the floor cleaners to the highest executives, has the power to stop the production line if they see a problem. This policy creates empowered employees who feel part of a larger mission. Our CANI process encourages employees to submit process change suggestions. They must identify the process, the suggested change, and the first- and second-level consequences of the proposed change. They then review this in their weekly team meetings. By the end of a new employee's first month, they are required to submit a CANI. If they're struggling to come up with one, they must ask for help. This fully integrates them into their work and helps them feel part of the bigger picture, which is particularly important for millennials.

This is also a matter of motivation. Even though we have distinct and carefully developed processes, our people are not cogs in a machine. They are smart, conscientious, and thinking individuals. These programs are designed to ensure that employees never feel like cogs. They give our people autonomy and the voice to change things, whatever their position. As Daniel Pink so keenly observes in his book *Drive: The Surprising Truth about What Moti-*

vates Us, "Control leads to compliance; autonomy leads to engagement."

These two tactics—The 30-Day Email and CANI—are not used to shame new employees for making mistakes or encountering challenges. They're about improving processes, which are not fail-proof. We want to make things good, then make them better, and analysis from fresh eyes helps us do that. More importantly, it encourages the new employee to be present in their work. It helps them feel like more than just cogs in a wheel. They are active participants in their processes, and they have a voice. They can speak up and share their honest experiences. They can fail, and we will work together to make failure less likely the next time around. So often companies tell people, "Do your work this way because that's how we do it." But we're all human, and we may have made a mistake when we established the "right way" of doing a task. At our firm, we're not about *being* right; we're about *getting it* right. These rituals ensure we hear an employee's voice, constantly improve our systems, and extend the excitement of joining our firm. New hires feel excited to be part of a group—a cult, if you like—that values their presence.

MAINTAINING EXCITEMENT

It's challenging to maintain the initial new job excitement beyond the first ninety days. People become acclimated to the firm's way of doing things, and the rhythm of life dulls the energy. To let employees refresh their energy and enthusiasm, we offer unlimited paid time off to salaried staff. They can take as much paid vacation time as they want. Of course, we must track it, but only lightly. People outside our firm tend to think this policy is unnecessarily generous. They roll their eyes at me, pitying my poor naiveté and imagining how much my employees take advantage of us. I don't usually admit that we implemented it because we were so sick of tracking this shit. It was a huge hassle to monitor days worked, vacation time accumulated, holidays used, and running balances of remaining paid time off for all our salaried staff. I was trepidatious about introducing this policy, but it has become much more than just a headache-saver. The two attorneys who take the most vacations are also our two best performers.

After an employee takes a paid vacation, they come back refreshed. They're more energized and ready to take on new challenges. They take pride in a job in which they feel autonomy because their boss isn't looking over their shoulder dictating where and when they spend their time. And they don't take advantage, either. These are good people who we don't have to watch over with a magnifying glass. We hired the right people into the right seats, and now have people of great character and morals who want to do right by us. They're not taking six weeks of vacation at our busiest time, then blaming us when work falls through the cracks. They don't shrug their shoulders and say, "Well, you're the ones who introduced unlimited paid time off. It's your problem if the work doesn't get done." No, these people take care of their shit. They know their responsibilities and respond to them. They do the right thing. They plan for their vacations. They balance their time off with other team members. They answer their phone at the top of the Eiffel Tower if they must. They also protect their colleagues. I once asked a team member, "Hey, where's Iana? I need to get hold of her." Iana's colleague said, "She's on vacation. What do you need? I'll help. I don't want to bother her." Good people protect their colleagues' space and appreciate the same in return.

It's taken me a long time to be okay with this idea. I come from an old-school work ethic. There's an old Dunkin' Donuts commercial in which a guy wakes up at some stupid hour like 3 a.m. He jumps out of bed and says, "It's time to make the donuts!" That's me. I get up and immediately want to work. I want to make the donuts before doing anything else. As I got older, I realized I was doing this wrong. You need to prioritize rest as much as work. You have to take a breather now and then. Millennials have the right idea here. When you give yourself a break, you can come back stronger and with more stamina. The same is true for your employees.

THE RIGHT PEOPLE FOR THE POLICY

Offering unlimited paid time off only works when you have the right people in the right seats. Before we nailed our hiring process, we tried to implement similar policies that fell flat. We had a self-care initiative that just ended in lies. I planned it after reading that people in service positions need time to focus on themselves. With workers' compensation, our clients all have injuries, and frontline staff almost act as social workers, helping these clients through difficult times. I read a study in *Harvard Business Review* that said some companies offer front-facing staff a break by sending them to volunteer at a homeless shelter or something similar. They think it's a fulfilling activity that will recharge the employee. In reality, our employees are already helping people every day, just in a different setting with a different set of problems. A real break would be to shift the focus from helping others to caring for themselves.

Based on this study, we put together a program in which we rewarded employees for reaching specific goals with up to four extra paid days off a year, one per quarter. They were to use these days for self-care. This felt particularly important as we had a lot of single mothers working for us, and they had no time for themselves. None. So I'd sit these employees down and ask, "When you were seven years old, what did you want to do for a living?" Inevitably, they did not answer, "I wanted to be a paralegal."

They dreamed of being a painter or a dancer or some other artistic, imaginative thing. I encouraged them to spend their reward days painting or dancing, going to a museum, or getting a massage. They could do anything that counted as self-care or personal development, but they weren't to spend the days running errands or numbing themselves with television, for example. It didn't work well. A couple of people went to an art museum. Others claimed they were doing self-care activities, but we were sure they were lying. It became a game for them to sneak around. We abandoned the program.

At that time, we hadn't hired people who shared our value of development or self-care, so employees weren't on board with our efforts. We also didn't have the right supervisors in place to support our goals. We had fallen victim to The Peter Principle. This is the scenario in which a person is promoted thanks to great success in their previous role, but they are incompetent in a more senior position, which requires a different skillset. They end up sitting in a job they aren't right for, too afraid to ask for help. Companies don't have enough guts to make a change when they realize their mistake, as they inevitably do, so a significant number of people end up languishing in unsuitable positions. How many people in your firm are not in the right seats? Ten percent? Twenty? Fifty? None of these percentages are unheard-of. The Peter Principle is rampant in US companies. If your firm suffers from the right people in the wrong seats, you must move them. Shift them to a more appropriate position or help them find a more fulfilling job elsewhere.

LET GO OF THE WRONG PEOPLE

Starting a job is a memorable life experience, and so is leaving one. No matter the terms of departure, it can be challenging for the firm and the departing employee. However, letting go of the wrong people is vital for business growth. I've yet to encounter a company perfect in its hiring. Often, the wrong people make it through the door. It's also common for the right people to end up in the wrong seats via The Peter Principle. When this happens, you must confront the brutal facts. They are holding the company and themselves back from growth. They are not the right person in the right seat. You must be brave, move quickly, and let them go—either into a new role or out of the firm entirely.

For a company that cares for its people, this is particularly difficult. We love our team and moving someone out is the hardest thing we have to do. We try everything possible before asking them to leave, including coaching and support. When we have fired someone, we've later realized it was best for everyone involved. We've seen the employee in question breathe a sigh of relief, knowing they aren't a good fit for the role. They likely are unhappy to lose their job, but it relieves the stress of struggling every day with tasks they cannot, or will not, complete. The more you hire people whose values match yours, the less you will have to worry about firing people. But once you know someone is not a fit, you have to get them out. This will free up an enormous amount of time for you to focus on managing processes, not people.

CHAPTER NINE

MANAGE PROCESS, NOT PEOPLE

"The moment you feel the need to manage somebody,
you've probably made a hiring mistake."

—JIM COLLINS

Here's a scene we played out hundreds of times in our firm's early days: An attorney would march up to his paralegal and say, "Mr. Jones called for an update on his case. I can't find his file. Where is it? Where's the damn file?" He and the paralegal would sift through the filing cabinet until they came across it. The attorney would open the file, and loose papers would spill onto the floor. "I can't find anything," he'd say. "Why is this such a mess?" And the paralegal would look at him and think, *Because you're the last one who touched it, and I didn't have time to reorganize everything after you screwed it up.* Supposedly simple tasks like pulling a file were chaos 90 percent of the time.

Clients couldn't get an update on their case in a reasonable time. They'd be on hold forever while attorneys and assistants battled with poorly organized files. Many times, clients couldn't even get through to us on the phone in the first place. We couldn't get our shit together enough to even answer calls. We had more business than we could manage, and clients were unhappy. This wasn't how we wanted to run our firm, so we started to look at our processes. What was involved in answering the phone and what prevented it from happening reliably? Who put files away and where? How could we make things less frustrating for attorneys, paralegals, and clients? Workers' compensation cases are very labor-intensive, so we started making incremental changes to reduce the frustration in that work.

Now, we manage our processes very closely. There are documented procedures for everything from onboarding new employees, as we discussed in the previous chapter, to client intake, opening, scanning, and distributing the mail, and even getting the company cars washed. We have time to focus on these processes because we're not busy managing employees. With the right people in the right seats, we don't have to spend time and energy coercing them into doing their damn jobs. Instead, we get to coach these good people to greatness. We manage process, and we coach people.

MANAGING VERSUS COACHING

Managing people requires a lot of effort. You're chasing them to find out why they came in late that morning or took a long lunch. You're constantly on their backs because they haven't completed projects on time or done things your way. However, when you hire the right people, they're motivated to show up on time and do the work without you harassing them.

Jim Collins instructs leaders to "hire motivated people and do your best not to demotivate them." If you give good people grief every time they step away from their desks, they will become demotivated. Instead, trust them. If they arrive late to work, trust that it's for unavoidable reasons. Hiring professionals, whether attorneys or mailroom staff, means you'll have an office full of people who can handle their shit. Good people don't need a manager to watch over their every move. They'll stay after 5 p.m., find ways to be more efficient, or enlist help. They'll do the right thing.

This doesn't mean you leave your staff stranded. Instead of managing, good leaders *coach* their employees. Managing is telling people what to do; coaching helps them do it. A manager sits behind staff while raising a whip, shouting, "Mush! Mush!" A coach stands in front, looks back at the team, and says, "Follow me." They are very different leadership techniques. A great leader cares for their employees by encouraging them to rise to their full potential and coaching them to create a better version of themselves. They help people master their work and progress to a higher level of fulfilled human needs.

Coaching requires you to care for the person being coached. Caring comes first. You might have all the legal knowledge, but unless employees know you care about them, their success, and their future, they won't want to work for you. As Brené Brown says, "Nobody cares how much you know until they know how much you care."

I have always cared deeply about those I work with, but I've often struggled to show it. For a long time, I didn't know how to talk to people. I spoke with employees the same way my father talked to me. He was an entrepreneur with many different businesses but, at heart, he was a comedian. I'm certain his real dream was to be a Catskill comic. He made jokes at every opportunity, which were always laden with sarcasm. In Brown's book *Dare to Lead* I read that the Latin root word for "sarcasm" translates as, "to tear flesh." At its most profound level, sarcasm is about tearing people apart.

Initially, I used a lot of dry humor and sarcasm at work. I eventually learned you can't do that. You must take the jokes out. I'm not saying you can't have fun, but you cannot laugh at other's expense. Those jokes are usually politically incorrect, but this isn't about being soft or avoiding getting sued. It's a question of motivation. Do you want to pump people up? Are you trying to motivate, encourage, and make them better people? Then don't tear them down on the other side by poking fun at them.

COACH WITH APPRECIATION

Aside from watching your jokes, you must also care for employees by openly appreciating them. This requires more than the occasional, bland "thank you." That's not enough. Perhaps it ought to be, but it never is. You could thank them one hundred times in a row, and it won't make an impression. Then one day, you'll criticize them for some small thing, and they'll remember that comment for years. It's human nature to disregard the positive and cling to the negative. You must be more creative in conveying your appreciation for employees, so it has a better chance of sticking.

The best way to show appreciation is by simply spending time with your team. Interacting on a social level has an incredible effect. Sam Walker wrote about this in his book *The Captain Class: The Hidden Force that Creates the*

World's Greatest Teams, which was ranked one of the top business books of 2017 by both CNBC and *The New York Times*. Walker tells the story of Tim Duncan, former captain of the San Antonio Spurs basketball team. Duncan was a very quiet guy who still made an effort every day to chat with as many people as possible in the Spurs organization, not just the players. He was, as Walker puts it, a captain in the organization. He made small talk. He socialized. He asked about kids and meatloaf recipes and injured ankles, and anything else in people's lives. He treated everyone there as a team member and showed his appreciation for their efforts by simply spending time talking.

I tell all our new team leaders to prioritize appreciating their team. Jason is an attorney who took this message to heart. He's a bit of a hippie, peace-and-love kind of guy. He also leads one of our top-performing teams. They're crushing their goals every month, and his staff just love him. I sat down with Jason one day to ask about his success.

"The team looks after each other," he said. "They're great people, we communicate well, and they care about our clients." In every word, Jason reflected his appreciation for the team. It was like he'd formed a habit of expressing gratitude toward them. Some of our other teams have struggled with this. As we learn from books like *Captain*

Class, every team needs someone like Tim Duncan who will be at the center of the team dynamic, spending time with teammates and ensuring things get done. In our firm, this team center is sometimes an attorney like Jason, but often they are not. Their job title is less important than their ability to focus on the team's soft skills in addition to practical aspects such as trial skills and knowledge of law. We've found that every good team has at least one person with exceptional communication, people skills, and the drive to simply get the job done. When a team has two such people, it really thrives. If a team has many of these types of people, it excels beyond belief. It is not usually the legal skills that determine a team's potential; it is people skills and a drive to do great work. As Walker also demonstrates in his book, every great team has great captains. Bilal and I are the overall leaders of our firm, but it is the team captains that really make us successful. Find these people, hang onto them, and let them know they are appreciated.

COACH PERSONAL GROWTH

Personal growth, as we discussed in chapter two, leads to self-actualization—the peak of Maslow's hierarchy of needs. Just as a football coach helps players improve their skills, a leader should coach employees to improve their capabilities. This isn't about coercing people into performing better; it's about offering the opportunity to fulfill the human need for growth. And you can't grow a business without growing individuals.

If you encourage growth, a team member will feel comfortable saying, "I think Janet's job is fascinating. How can I get there?" You, the coach, can then say, "Well, let's talk about Janet's job compared to yours. Janet uses these skills...This is what you'll have to focus on to get into that position. Let's develop an ascension plan for you to get there."

For lawyers, coaching to develop personal growth is particularly important. They can end up doing the same cases year after year, using the same old skills. Once they're up to speed in their area of practice, they get stuck on repeat. It feels stagnant. They might consider leaving the company or even the industry, just for a change of scenery. They might feel they have nowhere to go and nothing new to look forward to. In our firm, though, we are coaching lawyers to lead larger teams and offices. A high-growth lawyer provides a firm with so many opportunities, as the lawyer learns to navigate human needs and culture.

One of our attorneys, Mike, came to us and asked, "What's next?" He wanted a new challenge. We made him the managing attorney in our new office in Concord, California. After a few months in that role, the culture out in the new office seemed flat and uninspired. Several of the people there came from the Oakland office and really missed their old coworkers. Our Scorpion account manager, Evan Patlian, came to town for a strategy meeting, and we took a drive to the new Concord office. Evan has been our account manager for several years. He's a young man who has spent a good deal of time learning about sales and motivation from great authors like Seth Godin and Daniel Pink. He has counseled many great law firms on their marketing and business strategy. I shared my concerns with him, and after spending a few hours at the Concord office, he offered some sage advice.

"You have to break the new office from Oakland. Let it grow its own culture," he said. "Let them develop their own team and group dynamic and build their own examples of your company values." This was great advice. Bilal and I brought Mike into the mix and started coaching him on how to jump-start the culture.

Now, the Concord office has its own initiatives, happy hours, and even a movie night. I recently saw a note on our company-wide messaging platform about "stretching sessions." Sergio, who joined us shortly before his father's passing, leads the Wellness Program there, and it includes 2 p.m. stretching sessions which encourage employees to get away from their desks, move their bodies, and reenergize in the afternoon.

Mike developed a set of values for the Concord office that fall under the umbrella of the larger firm's values. In many ways, separating from the Oakland office and building their own subculture has been the best thing that could have happened. Mike himself has certainly moved into a new and challenging phase of his career.

DISCIPLINE IS CULTURE, AND CULTURE IS DISCIPLINE

Mike took our advice and ran with it. He needed some coaching, as we all do when faced with new challenges. However, we didn't have to watch over every aspect of the Concord office. We could trust Mike with it. This gives Irving and me time to manage processes. Businesses are simply a fabric of systems and processes designed to deliver value to clients. Disciplined, repeatable processes allow a company to grow. They let a company operate in a calmness rather than chaos. They are part of a strong culture. Managing processes involves looking to establish and improve those systems to constantly create better results.

We're not talking about documenting dress codes and overtime expectations. Those are policies to manage people. A thick policies manual suggests you've hired the wrong people—those who do not share your value of looking professional or working hard to get the job done. Procedure manuals are different. They deal with how to document case details, file with the court, intake a prospective client, and so on. We have procedures for everything down to how a client is greeted when they walk through the door. Deciding on and documenting these processes prevents a culture of frustration and creates a culture of productivity. It makes the business run faster, smoother, and fairer. And, at the risk of sounding morbid, it saves your ass if the one person with all the knowledge gets hit by a bus.

Whatever processes you create, they must be replicable. Even without the killer bus, replicable processes are essential for quality delegation and growth. This is what mega-companies like Starbucks have done. Starbucks, like all good companies, micromanages the customer experience so it can be replicated in any of their almost 30,000 locations. Every one of their baristas is on the same page, grinding beans, pouring espresso, and frothing milk the same way over and over again. The company's leaders have clearly envisioned their ideal customer experience, nailed their procedures, and communicated them to staff. Clear is important. And, as Brené Brown says, it is even more than that.

Brown's work on leading with courage and vulnerability in the workplace is simply brilliant. You must read her work. One of her concepts is simple, straightforward, and something we live by. She says, "Clear is kind. Unclear is unkind." When we get really clear in process and procedure and train people the same way in the same tasks, we get consistency. When we aren't truly and completely clear, we tend to leave it up to people to figure out processes for themselves. Then they get nervous. They don't know what to do and they hide the fact that they don't know. These secrets create a sense of insecurity. People want direction so they feel safer in executing their job. You have hired great people who want to do great work driving towards the company's vision. Only you can determine what that vision should look like and how you must execute processes to achieve it. If you can envision how clients should feel when they walk into the office, you must document and teach employees to greet clients in a way that will elicit those desired feelings. And if the process you teach doesn't work, as will sometimes be the case, you must give those involved the ability to change it. Be open. Put your ego aside and listen. Then be clear and kind in documenting and teaching your revised processes.

One of our core values is to deliver world-class customer service. We examine every procedure with an eye towards this goal, somewhat like Amazon's renowned "empty chair" exercise. Every meeting at Amazon includes an empty chair. The empty chair represents the customer. In every meeting, Amazon employees must ask themselves and each other what the customer in that chair would think. This empty chair exercise has helped us refine our processes so we can deliver curated, world-class customer service. This includes actions like greeting clients as they come into the office. The receptionist is prepared before they get there and knows their name.

"Oh, hi, you must be Mr. Mizuno," she says. They are brought to a conference room which was chosen the night before and set up with their name on a changeable office sign. "Client Meeting: Mr. Mizuno, 1 to 2 p.m.," it says. They are given reading material and a drink menu offering various coffees, teas, and waters. We developed this process to match our company's core value of world-class customer service. If that is also your value yet you can barely achieve a standardized way of answering the phone, you have some work to do!

Steve Jobs, the legendary CEO and co-founder of Apple, curated customer experiences through elegant design. Every detail of every Apple product is painstakingly designed. Even the products' unseen interiors are created with the same level of precision and beauty as the outside. Jobs was reportedly inspired by his father, a furniture maker who made certain that the back of all his furniture—the side against the wall—was just as beautiful as the side you saw every day. Every step in an Apple store, every curve of the iPhone, and even the interlocking circles on the box in which the Apple Watch is delivered, is designed to enhance the customer experience and represent the brand. Prior to Apple's introducing handheld products, consumer electronics came uncharged. What a letdown to the customer experience! Apple's team changed that. The moment you lift an iPhone from its box, press the power button, and see the screen light up is part of their curated experience.

Your job is to curate great moments for your staff and clients which properly represent your values, whatever they may be. This is not an easy task. In the firm's early days, we would get a few dozen phone calls a day and a handful of emails. A few months ago while reviewing data, I saw that we are now getting close to 20,000 text messages through our client text system and close to 5,000 phone calls in a single month. That's an average of almost 1,200 communications every business day. The processes that worked for us in the early days are no longer viable. We are constantly reviewing and refining our processes as we grow to ensure the team and client experience are world-class, as is our mission. We want to build something that delivers value in a special way, and that can endure seasons and years. This takes time, intense and thoughtful effort, and creativity. You and your team will also have to constantly review and refine your processes. Whether you're focused on the short-term success of just getting the phone answered the right way or on building a legacy, well-managed processes are essential.

COLLABORATE FOR SUCCESS

The best processes are managed collaboratively. They're designed and improved with input from those who work with them. You sit down and ask the mail person, "How can we make this better?" You can't sit on a lofty perch and dictate how to sort the mail. Instead, you bring your end goals to those involved and ask how best to achieve them. You say, "We want the mail to get to the right person the same day it arrives in our office. How can we do that?" Then use your listening skills from chapter three to really hear the mail person's ideas. When employees have control over their work and feel that their voices are valued, the best ideas surface.

If you don't believe your staff can provide valuable input into processes, there's a bigger problem at play. You either have the wrong people in place, or you are too distrusting to lead effectively. Lawyers can be cynical. We're trained to detect problems, cross-examine, and be argumentative. To be successful, though, you must set that aside, shut up during meetings, and listen to what your staff knows about daily experiences.

Paralegals and assistants are amazing people to involve in processes. We should include them because we're creating a culture-for-all, but they're also invaluable for any task to which a process can be applied. Long before my "cultural revolution," I read a book about how to grow profits through paralegals called *Paralegals, Profitability, and the Future of Your Law Practice* by Arthur G. Greene and Therese A. Cannon. The premise was that lawyers are expensive for a firm; paralegals are less so. If you can create manuals and binders full of well-managed processes, paralegals can execute the work. Firms save on operating expenses by reserving lawyer time for tasks only they can do. This makes financial sense, and it also removes friction from operations. Our lawyers are rarely in the office. They're in depositions, court appearances, and trials. When a client calls in, they're likely to speak with an assistant or a case manager—which is what we call our paralegals. We knew it was important for non-lawyers to be able to find case details, understand processes, and answer questions. They had to be more than message takers. We wanted them to connect with clients and truly be part of the process of serving justice, for their satisfaction and that of our clients.

MANAGING PROCESSES, NOT MICROMANAGING PEOPLE

I want to make a distinction between carefully managing processes and micromanaging people. Process management is essential to create a well-running firm. Micromanaging means having good people in place but constantly overseeing their every move. Micromanaging is interfering to the extent that employees cannot be themselves at work. In an effort to prevent failures, a micromanager creates an inhuman culture.

However, when someone does fail, it's an opportunity to improve the process or coach the person. Failures make people—and companies—stronger. It's like a broken bone fusing together with more than its initial strength.

It's hard to release the reins of managing people and coach them instead. Defining your values and getting the right people in the right seats makes it easier. That's when you stop flustering over disorganized files and missed phone calls. Time almost magically appears, allowing you to define and document processes. Your team members can follow those processes, fail occasionally, learn, and improve, which are all essential to a firm's growth.

CHAPTER TEN

A CULTURE FIT FOR GROWTH

"The best cases don't go to the best lawyers;
they go to the best marketers."

—MICHAEL MOGILL

We recently filmed a promotional video for the firm, and a former client offered to tell the camera crew about his experience with us. He'd talked about the great job we did getting his treatment covered and resolving his case. After the director interviewed him, the crew wanted to film B-roll—the supplemental footage they include of people laughing, the sun setting, and other basic shots. The client and I sat on a picnic bench in the small, grassy area outside our office and waited for the crew to finish shooting. As we sat, we talked. I asked him why he chose us. He said there were a few reasons, one of which was that he could feel our company culture even before he called. He'd worked for one company for many years and loved the owners and the culture there. Then, a private equity firm bought the company, and everything changed. No one seemed to care about the employees anymore. He could see from our website that we were a company that cared. So, he called our office and *he felt cared for*. Someone picked up the phone, listened to his story, and made him feel heard. That's why he used our firm for his workers' compensation case.

I know the team member who took his initial call. It was Almarie, our intake manager. She's one of our best people. She won the Foxhole Award the previous year for being the person other employees most want to work with. She makes her colleagues and clients feel safe, like she cares about them and has their back. She listens well. She's a tremendous person, so I wasn't surprised that the client felt there was a real person on the end of the phone who cared for him. Like all clients in the workers' compensation field, he came to us in a vulnerable position. He was suffering at the hands of an insurance company that had denied him treatment. He was unable to work and provide for his family. Almarie immediately made him feel he could breathe again. She removed much of his anxiety.

Hearing his experience, I was incredibly proud of Almarie and the firm. For years, we'd been working toward a positive company culture that would allow us to grow and serve our clients well. We'd determined our mission—to provide world-class service to the injured workers of our community. We'd hired people who shared our values, and we tried to live into those values every day. I finally felt like our values of acting with empathy, being vulnerable enough to really listen, and being driven to deliver world-class service weren't just words on a wall. They were real, and clients felt it.

A HUGE RESPONSIBILITY

Businesses that survive understand the role of each of its parts. Leaders lead, assistants assist, intake specialists process newly signed clients, the IT person does computer stuff, and the janitor empties the trash. The business, as an entity, is responsible for generating clients. This is an accepted truth for almost every type of business. In the legal field, however, attorneys are the ones traditionally expected to generate business for a firm or risk losing their jobs. I don't know why our industry is such an oddity. Perhaps, long ago, a bunch of bad marketers couldn't handle law firm accounts and just gave up, telling attorneys, "We don't know what we're doing. You guys do it."

Not only are the firms—which are businesses—opting out of marketing and, instead, charging attorneys with the responsibility, but they are expecting attorneys to find work without advertising. You can't name an automobile maker, airline, beverage company, or insurance provider that doesn't constantly plaster you with ads. However, I know of very few law firms that spend any money on advertising. From what I've seen, most spend nothing at all, unless you count the couple of hundred dollars required to host an outdated website. The handful of attorneys who do advertise spend a monstrous amount on it. Thanks to them, the law industry is one of the top advertising spenders, not quite at the levels of the automotive or pharmaceutical companies, but close.

So, a tiny percentage of law firms are buying a massive amount of advertising, while the vast majority seem to feel it's below the dignity of the profession. Years ago, law firms were prohibited from advertising. The rule was to protect vulnerable people. Eventually, the world realized that even vulnerable people need help finding services they want, and the prohibition was lifted. The stigma remains, though. I still know many lawyers who think it's awful for firms to advertise themselves. They are the ones whose attorneys promote themselves through speaking events and networking groups. There's nothing wrong with these forms of marketing; they can be extremely effective. However, firms cannot grasp that those *are* methods of marketing that are assigned to attorneys, not leaders.

MARKET THE MISSION, SHOWCASE THE CULTURE

Like any other business, law firms must market themselves. Our firm advertises on billboards, the radio, television, and online. We do it all. We've sponsored events, concerts, and all sorts of imaginative things. We're a mission-driven organization, like most law firms are, and it's essential that our marketing reveals our mission. The best marketers have been doing this for a long time.

Coca-Cola probably figured it out before anyone else. They've never sat around saying, "We sell sugar water!" No, they sell happiness, and spreading happiness is their mission. This is a fantastic marketing message because it makes them likable, and people want to do business with companies they like. This is especially true in today's culture where individual consumers can connect with mega-brands directly through social media. No one wants to work with robots; they want real people behind the interactions.

We bring our mission and culture to our marketing. Our website's home page states why we're in business. We have another web page that discusses our values. Marketing your culture isn't taking advantage to make a buck; it's honestly explaining what you're about as a firm. In chapter one, we talked about 360-culture, which is the idea that your company's culture influences the lives of everyone with whom it interacts. That includes prospective clients. They should know you are good people who are proud to work in a great environment.

That environment, shaped by your culture, is your key marketing advantage. Every law firm website in existence says, "We're the best." In fact, I've yet to run across one that says, "We're second-best." So how do you differentiate yourself from all the "best" firms around? You market your mission and showcase your culture. Within your mission, you will inevitably find details of how you effect change in your clients' lives. Our mission is to be the industry leader in plaintiff's workers' compensation law by providing world-class service to our clients, our team, and our community. This means we focus on these various aspects in our marketing, whether that's showcasing how we do things differently, how we impact our community, or how we focus on our people. Some of our mission-driven taglines are "Your fight is our fight," which evokes a sense of community and togetherness, and "Changing lives one client at a time," which speaks to the individual impact of our world-class service. Whether you're a workers' compensation firm like us or dealing with divorces, lawsuits, DUIs, car accidents, or small business litigation, we all work with people in vulnerable situations. They're still judicious enough to see law firm advertisements and make sensible, informed decisions.

Their circumstances, though, make it imperative that we treat them with care and empathy. That means we must treat clients exceptionally well, and that is the best marketing. It results in return business and word-of-mouth referrals.

This is vital, as there is serious and significant competition out there. Law firm advertising dollars may be consolidated to a few larger advertisers, but they are highly active. Their commercials fill the airways on television and radio. Their billboards line the highways. Pay-per-click ads via Google, Yahoo, and Bing flood the internet. Amidst all this, you must find ways to stand out. Marketing expert Seth Godin, whose blog is one of the most popular on the entire internet, says, "In a crowded marketplace, fitting in is a failure. In a busy marketplace, not standing out is the same as being invisible." Part of our goal in marketing our culture is to showcase a *likable* company that the broader consumer can *connect with*. Our client base loves knowing that we were named a "great place to work," as they come from places which are decidedly not so; they are, after all, seeking to sue for workplace injuries. It is not an accident that they know this about us. We advertise it.

You can't fake a caring culture. The public can see inauthenticity in a second. You must focus on building a great culture first, and marketing second—which is why this discussion falls toward the end of this book. As Peter F. Drucker famously said, businesses are nothing more than "strategic innovation and marketing." If you attempt to market a positive culture before you actually have one, clients will feel it. Don't make marketing promises you can't keep. They'll turn to the slew of review sites that let them share their experience and have no qualms about shaming you. If you have built your culture first, though, it would be a mistake to omit it from your marketing. Sharing your culture with prospects can grow your firm exponentially.

DON'T FEAR GROWTH

At a cocktail party a while ago, I ran into an old friend who's also an attorney. It had been years since we'd seen each other, and she asked what I was doing these days. I told her I ran a workers' compensation firm, and she asked how many people we had.

"About forty," I said. Her eyes widened.

"Oh my God! I can't imagine. That must be horrible," she said. I've had enough similar conversations with law firm owners to know she imagined there was an insane amount of work involved in managing everything. As we know, though, coaching good employees takes far less time than managing them. I tried to explain that building our firm is the best thing I've ever done, but I don't think she believed me.

So many lawyers fear growing their firms. They want more money but dread an unmanageable workload, and they aren't confident enough to hire good help. I once got talking to an attorney about marketing.

"Oh yeah, we tried that marketing thing once," he said. "We got all these calls from people who wanted to hire us."

"What did you do with those leads?" I asked.

"Well, I couldn't call everybody back, so I just kind of lost track of them," he said.

"Why didn't you hire help?" He looked at me like I was the idiot here.

"Then you have to train them," he said. Well, yeah, you do. But what's the alternative? Stagnation or, worse, closing your doors! If you want profits to grow, you must let your firm grow. That doesn't mean you, the leader, will be busier. If you build a strong culture, you'll get the right people into the right seats, and they will care for your clients, while you care for them.

As we've grown, our firm caseload has certainly increased.

We now handle 1,500 or more cases at any given time, and we have every intention of doubling and then tripling that number. I have not had to care for all these clients by myself. I know few of their names. That's not my job. As the leader, I'm required to care for our staff. *That* is my role. We have great people managing the caseloads, and they know the clients' names, their kids' names, their hobbies, and so on.

I do this by keeping the culture strong and bringing business in the door. Then our staff care for the clients and the clients care for all of us. This trickle-down effect means I am far less busy now with 1,500 clients and fifty employees than when I worked solo.

CHOOSE YOUR RELATIONSHIP

When you build a law firm with a strong culture, you get to choose the relationship you'll have with the business. Some people want to be a trial lawyer. Others, like me, focus on building a firm and coaching the next generation of leaders that can take over the firm. Many people dream of earning money while spending forty hours a week on the golf course. You get to choose. Once you're clear on what you want, find people to fill the other roles. While I'm thinking about business strategies and developing our culture, my partner, Bilal, practices law and levels up in his arena. That fulfills him. When he is not leveling up in his practice, he spends time visioning out the next phase of the firm when he and others will take the helm.

Your relationship with your business may change over time. There may be periods of flux when you want or have to work eighty hours a week, and times when you need to rest and take real, disconnected vacations. In my previous life, I consistently did eighty-hour workweeks without vacations. Now, I feel like I'm one hundred years old, because I powered through those earlier years and let my body crumble. I've now chosen a different relationship with work, where I can be in the office far less and jet down to Costa Rica to write this book. As I sit on a beach, brainstorming ideas, I know the business is still taking care of my family and me. I'm infinitely grateful that my team says, "Go write a book. Share what we've done here. Do what you want and take the time you need. We've got your back." This is thanks to the culture we've created, which lets me choose how I interact with the firm. They know I will always have their backs, too.

CHOOSE YOUR DAY, CHOOSE YOUR LIFE

Thanks to our success, I'm able to choose how my life runs from day to day. I still wake up early, usually between 4 and 5 a.m. I do some stretching and a bit of meditation, drink a bunch of coffee, and start working at home. My early morning work usually involves researching and reading about new software, marketing techniques, new markets for expansion, cultural trends, or new company initiatives, and considering how to implement these ideas. Then, when I'm not in Costa Rica (which is most of the time), I go to the gym for a few hours and head into the office. I usually have more coffee with Irving, our director of operations, just so we can say hello. I say hi to as many team members as I can find and invite someone to lunch. At lunch, I ask questions to gauge culture and satisfaction, and listen, really listen, to the responses. I spend afternoons in meetings and dealing with any issues. That's about it. I book very few phone calls and hardly have any emails to send.

That's why I can go to Costa Rica, help care for my aging mother, and spend time in the community. It's why I can spend time sharing our message of culture-first and culture-for-all, without my absence affecting income. We had our highest revenue quarter this year, with our highest ever profit margins. Within those three enormously successful months, I was away for more than five weeks. This works because we created a culture that doesn't revolve around me. It's a 360-culture in which all our team members are active. Bilal also gets to choose his relationship with the firm. He works hard as our managing attorney, and every year, he spends at least a month out of the office, which helps him relax and recharge. Since we began, he's been to Europe a few times, Hawaii, and Mexico. When he's out, his team covers him. They have his back. Even if you'd rather spend all your time in the courtroom, you need a 360-culture to support that. When you're in a four-week trial, you don't want to be distracted with small office issues. A strong culture will free you to focus on your case, while everyone else takes care of their shit.

Don't be afraid of growth. Market your mission and showcase your culture. If it's genuine, prospective clients will connect with your advertising. Then, clients will feel nothing but gratitude for delivering services in a way that aligns with your marketing. When I met that former client while we filmed B-roll for our promotional film, he was so thankful for our work. Really, though, he appreciated us fulfilling our promises. Advertisements are promises. *We promise we'll work our hardest for you. We promise we'll fight for your justice. We promise we care.* Don't be afraid to advertise the promises you make through a deliberately cultivated culture.

CONCLUSION

FOCUS ON FUNDAMENTALS

"It is not only less expensive to design culture early;
it will keep the company on track as it matures."

—JOSH LEVINE

John Wooden is arguably the best team sports coach in history. He led his basketball team, the UCLA Bruins, to ten national titles in twelve seasons from 1964 to 1975, including seven straight seasons from 1967 to 1973. UCLA went undefeated a record four seasons, winning eighty-eight straight games. When asked how he did it, Wooden said, "We focused on fundamentals. We practiced dribbling, passing, and shooting the ball. Nobody else does that."

Embracing your staff's inherent human needs and treating them well might seem too fundamental to make a difference. However, getting the basics right is the best way to win the game. When Bilal and I started our firm, we spent time figuring out how to make sure the phone was answered every time it rang, within three rings. We created processes for simple shit like returning calls on time and keeping the conference room clean. We focused on the most basic business elements. Now, we are constantly working on improving that client service. We do not have it all figured out. We get many, many things wrong. However, working hard on fundamentals has brought us a long way. It's distinguished us from others in our industry. Very few law firms understand the importance of these basics. Practice the fundamentals in this book and take it step-by-step. Stoic philosophy says work is a series of tasks, a trickle, a waterfall with no end. That's what will build your business—a trickle of incremental improvements that build into a culture that is bigger than the sum of its parts.

With the ideas in this book, you can reconnect with the original mission that compelled you to study law. You can embrace the humanity of your workplace with a culture-first and culture-for-all attitude. You can care for your staff's basic human needs, starting with physiological requirements, such as paying enough to cover basic needs for them and their family. You can ensure employees feel physically safe and emotionally secure enough to show up at work as their whole selves. You can create a disciplined, predictable, and productive workplace in which employees trust. You can create a place where people feel the safety of social acceptance. You can meet their esteem needs and help them grow as individuals. You can learn to listen and get in touch with your current culture and be grateful for whatever you discover. You can adopt your personal values into your company and envision what that will look like for your firm.

You can learn that ego is the enemy, as Ryan Holiday so insightfully said. When you remove ego from the equation, you become able to listen and vulnerable enough to admit you don't know everything. Vulnerability creates space for true connection with the staff who serve your clients. You can heed the call of self-care, which is the only way to survive the intensity of running a business. You can find a hobby. Hobbies generate energy and clear the mind. A clear mind is a breeding ground for creativity, and creativity creates business growth. You can harness the superpower strength of being calm. You can actively listen to your team and their needs and choose to react only to what matters. You can be a great manager and agent of change. Being willing to change in this way made me a true leader, and it will do the same for you.

You can avoid desperation hiring and instead approach hiring with patience, only allowing the right people in the door. You can find positive employees with grit and good character, whose values match your own. You can enact processes to deliberately employ those with transferable soft skills and a desire to grow. When necessary, you can let a seat sit empty until the right candidate arrives. And you can be open to hiring millennials, who are mindful and willing to bring their whole selves to work. Remember: millennials are the future.

Once you have the right people in the right seats, you can celebrate their life experiences. Let their first day be indicative of how much you care for your staff. You can curate the onboarding experience, so new hires feel safe in their decision to join your firm. You can extend their excitement into the first ninety days and beyond with initiatives that show they are more than just cogs in a wheel. This lets them know they are appreciated and trusted. When needed, you can let go of the wrong people.

You can closely manage processes and collaborate with those who execute them to create constant improvements. You can resist the urge to manage your staff, and instead coach them to create a better version of themselves. You can help them master their work and become more fulfilled people. You can show you appreciate staff by spending time with them and paying attention to their personal growth—as a firm cannot grow without its people growing first.

You can accept that it is the company's responsibility to bring in business, and do so by marketing your mission and showcasing your culture. When you do this, your new culture will create growth. Do not fear growth; it is the path to freedom. It lets you choose your relationship with your firm. When your business grows, you can decide what your work and life will look like.

If you find success in implementing these ideas, share them with other lawyers. We can create a legal community with happier lawyers, more fulfilled support staff, and less stressed owners. We might not create rainbows and sunshine and world peace, but lawyers do something significant in this world. We fight for justice. We speak for those who can't speak for themselves. When we can do this work better, when our businesses are more profitable and sustainable, when our employees are fulfilled and able to fully care for clients, we can serve justice to more people and create legacies that outlive us.

On a more practical level, employees will love working for the mission. They'll proudly wear the T-shirts you give them, instead of using them as rags around the house. You'll have a bigger fan base, creating a tribe of clients who share your values. You won't have to live the stereotype of working eighty hours a week until you burn out. By focusing on culture, you can stop being a slave to your law firm, grow your practice, and actually be happy.

ACKNOWLEDGMENTS

I have to start by thanking my wife, Diana, for the constant stream of ideas, for reading these pages over and over, and for keeping me focused. Thank you for helping shape how this story is told—a story which, in many ways, is *our* story. More than anything, thank you for your love, support, and encouragement.

To my parents, Michael and Linda Farber. I wish my father were still here. He was an entrepreneur, and my mother was a chef and an artist. Together, they taught me that business is an art, carefully constructed with intense effort, wonder, imagination, and humanity.

To Bilal Kassem, my law partner, who did our first employee survey. It opened my eyes to the truth and forced me to dig deeper, to struggle, and to learn to do my job better. Thank you for making our partnership the easiest law partnership I know of. You have an amazing career ahead of you and hope you will carry on these ideals we have shaped together.

I want to thank Irving Flores-Corona, Karla Ortega, and Iana Zadneprovskaia—the original team still with us. Thank you for believing in us and dedicating years of your careers to seeing our mission through. To the rest of the team at Pacific Workers': Almarie Rodriguez, Miguel Espino, Ruben Amezquita, Jazmin Orozco-Salcedo, Michael Ullrich, Zachary Kweller, Samantha Malano, Sergio Ardila, Alison Gude, Carmen Ramirez, Jason Insdorf, Brenda Alvarez, Natalie Vasquez, Jocelyn Onofre, Brisa Aceves, Shane McKay, Yadira Piceno, Maria Gaytan, Patricia Gamez, Janet Alvarez, Jessica Pedroza, Darlene Jablonski, Marco Rodriguez, Karla Leiva, Jose Moreno, Luzdary Algood, Rosa Lemus, and Dulce Cruz. There is no better and more dedicated group of people who I would rather have with me in the foxhole. Every day, you set the example of our values and bring a better version of yourselves to work. We have built something special, and it will take care of all of us. A better me = a better you = a better us.

To Gil Alvandi, the student who became the master. Thank you for helping me make the change to the most rewarding chapter of my career. Thank you for the daily 5 a.m. calls, the encouragement, and the reminders that things will be okay when they felt deep and dark. Your counsel and friendship have been valuable beyond measure. They have helped me stay centered and focused. And thank you for the constant reminder that life is not always about building; sometimes, it's just about living your best life.

I have to acknowledge my closest friend, Allan Flader, who passed during the writing of these acknowledgments. Allan created an amazing culture for his small financial advising company. He was beyond kind, funny, open, warm, and generous. More than anything, he was dedicated to his family, his friends, his clients, and his community.

I want to leave what I wrote prior to his passing:

> To my closest friend, Allan Flader, and his wonderful wife, Katherine, who, as they go through their own deepest struggle, remain dedicated to family, friends, charity, and compassion for everyone. You are both truly wonderful people.

To my brother, Neil Farber, and my niece, Kaelah, for their sacrifice in caring for my mother at such an important time in her life. You have taken the worry from me. Every day, you make her life fun and interesting. Our family owes you both our gratitude for a debt that we can never truly repay.

To Leland Thompson, my coach and friend. You are an amazing individual. Thank you for all the counsel and the exchange of ideas, concepts, and books. I look forward to our next monthly dinner within minutes of the current one ending. You helped me through this journey of discovery by asking the right questions and, often, figuring out the answers. I greatly admire your positivity and discipline.

To Michael Mogill, the force of greatness long needed in the business of law. You and the Crisp team have done, and continue to do, amazing things. The company and culture you have built are incredible. I knew in the first few moments that we spoke that you are the one to watch in this business. Your ideas of what legal marketing and law firms are truly about are visionary. Most importantly, thank you for giving me the first stage to talk about law firm culture and encouraging me to get these ideas into a book and out to the legal world. I just wish you would keep your message down to a small roar—or my competition may find out!

To Donald David. Thank you for having faith in a young lawyer over twenty years ago. You gave me my first real chance on great clients and taught me what it truly means to be a lawyer.

I want to thank RJon Robins from How to Manage a Small

Law Firm for his insight and counsel. I may spread a small message, but you are out there every day sharing the grand message and helping people create amazing law firms and better lives for themselves. To all those nonbelievers: yes, it is possible!

Thank you to the team at Scribe and Lioncrest, including JT, Kacy, and Liz. Thank you, especially, to Liz for the incredible support, encouragement, and care. It is amazing to work with such incredible professionals.

Lastly, to all the solo and small firm lawyers out there. Remember: there is a different and better way to run your practice, so your practice doesn't run you!

ABOUT THE AUTHOR

ERIC FARBER is on a mission to change how law firms operate by showing lawyers the value of putting culture first. During his twenty-five years as a lawyer, Eric has lived the transformation from scarcity to abundance that becomes possible when you shift your perspective and prioritize people. As the CEO and chief legal officer of Pacific Workers' Compensation Law Center, Eric's focus on culture helped him build a seven-figure firm that's gone from four people to forty in just five years, been an *Inc.* 5000 company twice, was named to the Bay Area 100 list of fastest-growing companies, and spent two consecutive years in the top fifty of Law Firm 500.